THE BATTLE OF

Sirte

OTHER WORKS BY S. W. C. PACK

Anson's Voyage
Weather Forecasting
Admiral Lord Anson
The Battle of Matapan
Windward of the Caribbean
The Wager Mutiny
Britannia at Dartmouth
Sea Power in the Mediterranean
Night Action off Cape Matapan
The Battle for Crete
Cunningham the Commander

SEA BATTLES IN CLOSE-UP · 15

THE BATTLE OF
Sirte

S. W. C. PACK

LONDON

IAN ALLAN LTD

First published 1975

ISBN 0 7110 0596 6 -85/74

Published by Ian Allan Ltd, Shepperton, Surrey,
and printed in the United Kingdom by
Biddles Ltd, Guildford, Surrey

Contents

Maps

Preface and Acknowledgements

We are often accused of studying strategy and tactics that are out of date. Yet we are seldom admonished for repeatedly ignoring the lessons of history that recur with amazing regularity as the years pass.

Weapons and tactics are constantly changing, but strategical factors such as preparedness, flexibility, mobility, co-ordination, replenishment bases, the element of surprise, human morale, dedication to service, and, above all, the personal touch of the leader, can only be neglected at a nation's peril.

In the study of the Battle of Sirte I have found those books listed in the Bibliography most useful and I am grateful for permission to reproduce short comments made by the following:

Admiral of the Fleet Viscount Cunningham of Hyndhope, Kt, GCB, OM, DSO, in his *A Sailor's Odyssey* (Hutchinson 1951)
Admiral of the Fleet Sir Philip Vian, GCB, KBE, DSO, in his *Action This Day* (Muller 1960)
Vice-Admiral Sir Albert Poland, KBE, CB, DSO, DSC, in *Men of Action* by Kenneth Edwards (Collins 1943)
Captain E. W. Bush, DSO, DSC, in his *Bless Our Ship* (George Allen & Unwin 1958)

I am also indebted to the USNI, Annapolis, for permission to quote short extracts from Cdr M. A. Bragadin's *The Italian Navy in World War II* (USNI 1957), which I have used to preserve a balanced point of view.

I am particularly grateful for personal accounts of the battle which Lord Cunningham called the 'most brilliant action in the war'. They not only enliven the narrative, but form valuable testimony of events experienced at first hand long ago. My contributors are:

Rear-Adm I. G. Aylen, CB, OBE, DSC. (EO, *Kelvin*)
Capt E. W. Bush, DSO, DSC. (Capt, *Euryalus*)
Capt R. D. Butt. (Mid, *Jervis*)
Capt D. R. J. Edkins, the Hampshire Regiment (passenger in SS *Talabot*)
Rear-Adm R. L. Fisher, CB, DSO, OBE, DSC. (Capt, *Hero*)
Adm Sir Guy Grantham, GCB, CBE, DSO. (Capt, *Cleopatra*)
Capt C. A. G. Hutchinson, DSO, OBE. (Capt, *Breconshire* and Commodore of convoy)
Adm Sir Henry McCall, KCVO, KBE, CB, DSO. (Capt, *Dido*)
Rear-Adm St J. A. Micklethwait, CB, DSO. (Capt, D22, *Sikh*)
Lt-Col R. B. Moseley. (Staff of C-in-C)
Rear-Adm A. D. Nicholl, CB, CBE, DSO. (Capt, *Penelope*)
Capt Sir Aubrey St Clair-Ford, Bt, DSO. (Capt, *Kipling*)
Adm Sir Wilfrid Woods, GBE, KCB, DSO. (SOO to C-in-C)

I have taken some trouble over the maps in order to assist the narrative, but it must be remembered that positions and tracks of individual ships (on both sides) are somewhat subjective and often irreconcilable, so that some liberties have to be taken in combining them.

It is hoped that the facts and analyses in the various appendixes will prove interesting and valuable as a complement to the narrative. Readers may find the Chronology in Appendix D useful.

I am grateful for help received from Capt R. S. Falconer, RN, Mr J. D. Brown of the Naval Historical Branch Library, and from the Library of the Britannia R.N. College, Dartmouth.

For the large selection of photographs I am indebted to Messrs Brennan, Hine, and Squires of the Imperial War Museum; Mr Preston Grover; Admiral Angelo Iachino; the Italian Navy; Admiral Sir Henry McCall; and Rear-Adm St J. A. Micklethwait.

Above all I owe much to my wife for her endless encouragement and help.

Blossom's Pasture,   *S. W. C. Pack 1975*
Strete,
Dartmouth.

CHAPTER ONE

The First Battle of Sirte

When referring to The Battle of Sirte it is necessary to explain
that two battles were fought in the Gulf of Sirte. The first was
a brief encounter on December 17th, 1941. The second was
that which Admiral Sir Andrew Cunningham described as "one
of the most brilliant actions of the war", fought on March
22nd, 1942 between an Italian fleet of one battleship, two
heavy cruisers, and a light cruiser, against a British force of five
light cruisers. For warship particulars see Appendix B.

In general when reference is made to The Battle of Sirte, it
is the second battle that one has in mind, and it is the main
subject of this book. The first battle, however, the short
encounter, is briefly described in this chapter.

A glance at Map 1 will show the interdependence of various
regional operations, in 1941 and 1942, and the strenuous
activities on both sides to maintain supply lines. Each side
faced the essential need to replenish his tenuously held bases.
The Axis powers had to provide south-running convoys to feed
Tripoli, and any ports that they might possess further east in
support of General Rommel's drive eastward with his Afrika
Korps towards Egypt. Britain on the other hand had to restock
Malta by means of west-running supply ships from Alexandria,
and east running convoys from the United Kingdom via
Gibraltar, in order to sustain Malta's ability for offensive
action by sea and air against Axis convoys.

Fortunes swayed back and forth. When British attacks on
Italian convoys were successful, Rommel's supplies were in
jeopardy. And British retention of airfields in Cyrenaica then
enabled air defence and valuable reconnaissance information
to be given to British warships for their further efforts to
destroy Italian shipping and the supplies for Rommel's forces.

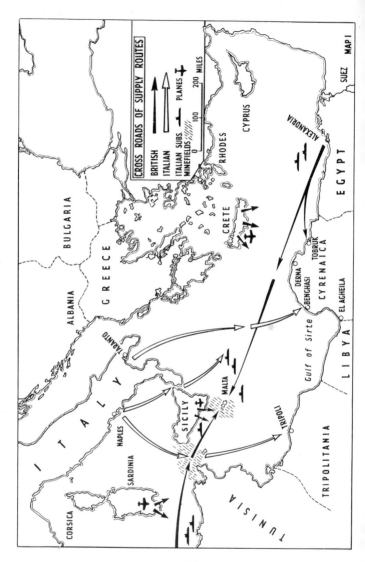

CROSS ROADS OF SUPPLY ROUTES

BRITISH
ITALIAN
ITALIAN SUBS.
PLANES
MINEFIELDS

0   100   200 MILES

MAP I

BULGARIA

ALBANIA

GREECE

ITALY

TARANTO

NAPLES

SARDINIA

CORSICA

SICILY

TUNISIA

TRIPOLITANIA

TRIPOLI

MALTA

RHODES

CRETE

CYPRUS

SUEZ

EGYPT

ALEXANDRIA

TOBRUK

DERNA

BENGHASI

CYRENAICA

EL AGHEILA

LIBYA

Gulf of Sirte

Also it was then easier to pass British convoys to Malta, and at times to replenish her dwindling air strength.

By the autumn of 1941 Britain appeared to be recovering from the effects of the heavy losses suffered off Greece and Crete in the spring, and a favourable trend was gathering momentum owing to the successful passages of British convoys through the Mediterranean. Hurricanes were successfully flown to Malta from the British aircraft carrier *Ark Royal,* and the island's strike capacity was improved by flying RAF bombers and naval torpedo-bombers into Malta. In addition, the newly formed 10th Submarine Flotilla based on Malta, which consisted of *Unbeaten, Unbroken, Upholder, Upright, Urge, Ursula,* and *Utmost,* names soon to become famous, began to exact a heavy toll from Italian warships and shipping. The German staff in Italy described those losses as "catastrophic", but they were modest compared with the wholesale destruction on November 8th, 1941, in the Straits of Messina, of a convoy of Axis supply ships bound for North Africa in support of Rommel. This was the work of Captain W. G. Agnew's famous Force K which was based on Malta, and operated in the dark hours of the night. In another night action, this time off Cape Bon, on December 13th, a flotilla of four British destroyers under Commander G. Stokes on the way to Alexandria to reinforce Cunningham's destroyers, sank two Italian cruisers carrying a deck cargo of petrol for Tripoli. The Italians had no proper facilities for night action, and discouraged as a policy the acceptance of night action.

Rommel's supplies had become dangerously short, and when the British Eighth Army struck on November 18th, 1941, his Afrika Korps suffered a severe defeat. By January 12th, 1942 Rommel had been forced back to the borders of Tripolitania and all Cyrenaica was once again in British hands, thanks not a little to the maintenance of British sea power and the destruction of Axis supplies at sea. But the situation was again to change markedly, due to the return of the Luftwaffe's Fliegerkorps II from the Russian front to Sicily, in December 1941, a step which was greatly to increase local German air superiority.

Also in the meantime a series of disasters had befallen the British fleet, first with the torpedoing of the aircraft carrier

Ark Royal on November 14th, and then the battleship *Barham* on November 25th. The cruiser *Galatea* was lost off Alexandria on December 14th. Five days later the cruiser *Neptune* of Force K sank after striking no less than four mines which had been skilfully laid by Italian destroyers 20 miles north-west of Tripoli. There followed the loss of the destroyer *Kandahar* which gallantly went to look for survivors.

But there were even worse disasters to come, for on the night of December 19th, 1941, three intrepid Italian submarines entered Alexandria harbour unobserved in their chariots, while British destroyers were passing through the open gate. They attached delayed-action mines to the battleships *Queen Elizabeth* and *Valiant,* which when detonated put the two ships out of action for months, thus in one fell swoop bringing about a dramatic change in the balance of naval power. The fact that Japan had entered the war less than a fortnight earlier, without a declaration of war, and had sunk the American battle fleet at Pearl Harbour, and three days later had sunk the British battleship *Prince of Wales* and the battle cruiser *Repulse,* added seriously to what had now become a very grave situation. The loss of Cunningham's heavy ships was in itself a severe blow for the British, since Italy still possessed four battleships; but the more serious aspect for Cunningham was that there was now no early prospect of receiving an aircraft carrier with all its advantages of naval reconnaissance, air defence for the fleet, and offensive strikes by torpedo-bombers.

Fortunately both the *Queen Elizabeth* and *Valiant* had settled vertically and in shallow water, so that it was some weeks before the enemy realised the full extent of their advantageous situation. Cunningham took every precaution to maintain the deception. But not since 1796, when Britain had withdrawn her fleet from the Mediterranean, had her Navy been so hard pressed; there was speculation at the Admiralty that a similar withdrawal might now be forced on her. Cunningham replied that Britain should beware of losing her position in the Mediterranean; and in keeping with his usual plea, he reiterated that retention must rest on adequate air striking power. His fleet had been without an aircraft carrier ever since *Formidable* had been disabled in May 1941, during the battle for Crete.

For a few weeks towards the end of 1941, each side with great urgency concentrated on getting its own convoys through, generally at the expense of offensive action, though each would inevitably have to endure air attacks.

What the Italians later called the first battle of Sirte, resulted from an attempt by the British in mid-December 1941 to send the fast supply ship *Breconshire* with much-needed fuel for Malta. She had completed many such missions for Alexandria and had remained unscathed.

Breconshire sailed from Alexandria late on December 15th, 1941 with an escort consisting of the anti-aircraft cruiser *Carlisle* and seven destroyers, in company with the two light cruisers of the 15th Cruiser Squadron, *Naiad* (flag) and *Euryalus*, all under the command of Rear-Adm Philip Vian.

The Italians were at the same time concerned in a supreme effort to get four large supply ships to Tripoli, and these left Naples on December 16th, escorted by light destroyers. They were taking no chances, and in anticipation of a possible meeting with Cunningham's battleships, (this was three days before the disabling of the *Queen Elizabeth* and the *Valiant*), had arranged for their four battleships to be at sea in covering support. In the event Cunningham found it quite impracticable to take the battleships to sea, because of the small number of available destroyers and the disproportionate number that would be required to act as an anti-submarine screen. There had been a screen of only eight destroyers when the *Barham* was torpedoed, and these had proved inadequate. Vian in consultation with Cunningham expressed a preference for available destroyers to be at hand with his new cruiser squadron, rather than allocated as a screen for the battle squadron; thus he would forego battleship support.

After dark on the 16th, the evening following his departure from Alexandria, Vian sent the *Carlisle* and two destroyers to the eastward with orders to chatter on their radio at midnight to convey the impression that the British battleships were also at sea. He knew by this time that his own force had been reported. On this same evening Force K, consisting of the cruisers *Aurora* and *Penelope,* and four destroyers, sailed

17

east-south-eastward from Malta in accordance with the plan that they should meet Vian on the forenoon of the 17th and then reverse course and take the *Breconshire* on to Malta. On learning of the Italian battleships at sea Cunningham ordered that Vian's force should remain in support of the *Breconshire* until dark on the 17th, and then after detaching her to Malta, attack the enemy with torpedoes.

Cunningham describes how "galling in the extreme" it was for him now, to remain fuming in Alexandria with his battle fleet immobilised for want of destroyers, and knowing that enemy battleships were at sea: the battleships that had eluded him so many times in the last eighteen months. A German plane had, however, reported earlier that day, the presence of a British force composed of "a battleship, two or three cruisers and a dozen destroyers" proceeding westward. The so-called battleship was possibly a mistaken identification of the large *Breconshire,* but this report led the Italians to believe that the British were planning to attack the important Axis convoy bound for Tripoli, a belief further strengthened by a reconnaissance report that Force K had left Malta.

Force K, the *Aurora* and *Penelope* with their destroyers, duly joined Vian on the morning of the 17th (see Map 2). Vian's combined force now steered a point or two south of westward, with the object of delaying interception by the Italians until dark if possible. They were subjected to constant air attacks by high-level bombers and torpedo-bombers, but received no damage. They were shadowed all the time. Cunningham complains of the lack of British air support and says that reconnaissance was unsatisfactory. However at 10.25 on the 17th came the expected report of enemy heavy forces to the northward, amplified further by a reconnaissance plane in the afternoon. This was part of the Italian supporting force consisting of the battleship *Littorio* flying the flag of the Commander-in-Chief, Admiral Iachino, the battleships *Doria* and *Cesare,* together with the heavy cruisers *Gorizia* and *Trento,* and 10 destroyers; all steaming south-westward. Further west of this heavy force by some 60 miles, and close to the Italian convoy, was the battleship *Duilio* with three cruisers and 11 destroyers, but this group were not reported.

Iachino received an air sighting of the British force at about

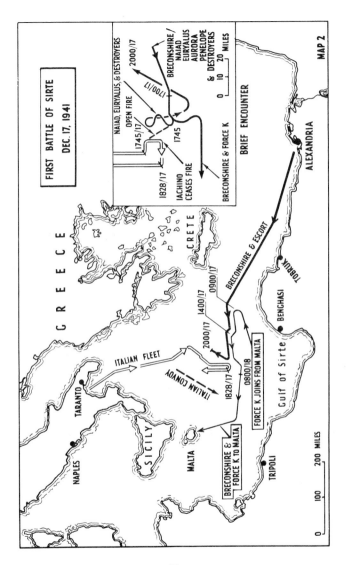

FIRST BATTLE OF SIRTE
DEC. 17, 1941

BRIEF ENCOUNTER

MAP 2

the same time, and, still under the impression that this force included a British battleship, turned with his three battleships and two cruisers to the southward and increased speed to 24 knots.

It was not until 17.45 that Vian, then in the middle of a heavy air attack, sighted Iachino's force 25 nautical miles to the north-westward. Iachino had already sighted him and had turned to the eastward, so Vian immediately detached the *Breconshire* and Force K to the southward at full speed, and boldly closed to attack the Italians with his small covering force. At 17.53 the *Littorio* opened fire with her modern 15in guns at a range of 17 nautical miles (32,000 metres), and the Italian heavy cruisers joined in with their 8in guns at maximum range. It was however, rapidly becoming dark, and Vian added to the difficulty of being spotted by laying down a smoke screen. He also sent in his destroyers for a torpedo attack under cover of the screen. A midshipman (now Captain R. D. Butt) serving in the destroyer *Jervis,* writes: "We came under unpleasantly accurate fire from the main armament of their battleship for a while, but were not hit. The 15in shells sounded like motor buses going overhead. The first lieutenant (Walter Scott) promised me a severe hiding if I mal-operated my searchlight during the sweep for the enemy; if we both survived".

By 18.04 it was already dark. Iachino ceased fire and turned away at speed. His ships had no radar and were ill fitted for any sort of night action or defence from destroyer assaults in the dark.

The encounter was over. It had lasted eleven minutes, and Iachino had not only failed to inflict much damage but had also allowed the *Breconshire* to continue safely on her way to Malta. Indeed he was still unaware even of her presence at sea. Vian, having sent on the *Breconshire* with Force K, returned with his covering force at high speed to Alexandria, on arrival at which his ships would need to replenish with fuel and ammunition.

Thus ended the brief engagement in the Gulf of Sirte which the Italians labelled the First Battle of Sirte. It was a tame affair compared with the Second Battle of Sirte, nevertheless the Italians regarded it as a great success, for they were able to get their own convoy safely into Tripoli. Moreover the encounter was immediately followed by a disaster for the British when Force K, having seen the *Breconshire* safely into Malta, and having refuelled there, set off at high speed with the cruiser *Neptune* in an attempt to intercept the Italian convoy. It was then that they ran into an Italian minefield which cost them the loss of the *Neptune* and the destroyer *Kandahar* as already described, and also serious damage to the *Aurora* and *Penelope*.

Despite the superior numerical advantage enjoyed by the Italians however, there is evidence of the continuing moral ascendancy exhibited by Cunningham's ships. Optimistically the historian Commander Bragadin writes of the Sirte encounter, in *The Italian Navy in World War II*, as being a complete success, and says "Not only was this a welcome change, but to add to the good fortune, the *Littorio* group had taken the offensive for a whole day against a British group and had forced it to retire".

CHAPTER TWO

In Adversity; Defiance

The year 1941 had ended with the relief of Tobruk by British troops, and a successful push westward which drove Rommel's Afrika Korps right out of Cyrenaica. Thus was restored once again to the British the possession of strategic airfields along the north coast from Alexandria to Benghazi, and the neutralisation of German air domination in "Bomb Alley". The Inshore Squadron whose primary duty had been the supply of the beleaguered garrison at Tobruk was now spared this duty and was able to operate much further west.

It might be thought that the entry of America into the war would have brought relief to British maritime forces, but the reverse was true and there was an intense shortage of shipping. The Japanese had effected acute, crippling measures in a very short time, added to which the Germans had greatly stepped up their U-boat campaign.

Cunningham's battle force had been severely depleted by the disasters of 1941, and recently by transfer of ships to other stations. Local air strength was also suffering through diversions to the far east. Still high on the list of responsibilities were the reinforcement of Malta, the supply and support of the British Desert Army, and the interception of Italian convoys running to Tripoli.

By January 6th, 1942 the British Army's determined drive westward was suddenly brought to a halt at Agadebia which borders the south-eastern region of the Gulf of Sirte. This was largely due to their outrunning supplies and also to a deterioration in the supply position because of the extension of the war to the far east. Meanwhile the Italians successfully sent in two convoys to North Africa consisting of considerable supplies for Rommel.

Never one to miss a chance, Rommel wasted no time in

preparing a lightning counter-attack, which he launched on January 21st. In two weeks he recaptured most of Cyrenaica. By February 7th, 1942 he had occupied Gazala and driven Auchinleck's army back to Tobruk. His left flank had been greatly supported by the Fliegerkorps II which had recently been transferred from the Russian front to Sicily. 'Bomb Alley' was once again dominated by the Luftwaffe. With Auchinleck in full retreat towards Egypt, the hard-worked little ships of the Inshore Squadron were again busy, this time evacuating men and equipment from abandoned ports.

The supply position for Malta was now becoming critical. The island itself was increasingly the object of attack by aircraft based only a hundred or so miles away in Sicily. The retention at Malta of surface ships of Force K, and submarines of the 10th Submarine Flotilla, was hazardous in the extreme, yet essential while the need to intercept Italian supplies to Tripoli continued. Cunningham told the First Sea Lord that he was "alarmed about Malta's supplies".

Nevertheless he was determined that fast supply ships should be sent from Alexandria, escorted as before by Vian's 15th Cruiser Squadron now consisting of the *Naiad, Euryalus,* and the *Dido,* strengthened by the anti-aircraft cruiser *Carlisle.* The *Dido* had returned in December 1941 after four months in America repairing damage sustained at Crete.

Early in January 1942, Cunningham had been able to send the fast fleet auxiliary HMS *Glengyle* to Malta with replenishments of oil, escorted by Vian's force until junction was made with Malta's Force K. Vian then escorted the empty *Breconshire* back to Alexandria. In the absence of any aircraft carrier, reconnaissance and fighter protection had been successfully provided by the Naval Co-operation Group No 201 of the RAF, an innovation which Cunningham had sought for a long time, and which had eventually been approved in December 1941. A further convoy was run in mid-January, and this time three ships out of four arrived safely. Towards the end of February, yet another successful operation was achieved, the *Breconshire* running into Malta and the empty *Glengyle* being brought safely back to Alexandria. Protection was again provided by the Naval Co-operation Group No 201, and Cunningham praised their efficiency. "It showed" he said, "what could be done with aircraft trained to work over the sea". The local air defence put up by Malta's Hurricanes was also commendable, but already the island was suffering from the increasing attentions of Fliegerkorps II, and as Rommel further established himself in North Africa the position began to look critical, Malta's small force of Hurricanes by now reduced to single figures. These Hurricanes had become inferior to the Me 109s of Fliegerkorps II, but at last Spitfires were being allocated by the Air Ministry in a late effort to save Malta. It only remained for the hazardous task of flying them into the island to be carried out from the old carriers *Argus* and *Eagle,* under cover of Force H operating from Gibraltar. The first attempt was frustrated by defects in the Spitfires' fuel tanks, but on March 7th, 1942, 15 Spitfires and seven Blenheims reached the island safely.

On February 12th Cunningham had again attempted to send a convoy to Malta, this time of three fast freighters under cover of Vian's cruiser squadron. But German Luftwaffe domination had defeated the attempt, two of the freighters being sent to the bottom, and a third, the SS *Clan Campbell* being forced by severe bomb damage to take shelter in Tobruk, still in British hands. This defiant effort was substantial, yet brought no relief at all to the beleaguered island. What was worse, the Italians successfully ran a large convoy of six freighters to Tripoli in late February, under battleships and cruiser cover, and escaped unharmed by British air efforts whose attacks, because of a series of accidents and erroneous reports, proved completely abortive. Nor were British submarines successful on this occasion. The truth was that in spite of defiant determination to turn the scales, the defenders of Malta were nearing the end of their tether. The arrival of a few more Spitfires on March 21st could do little more than raise hopes that air defence might continue a little longer. In the meantime the aircraft of Fliegerkorps II hammered away at Malta's airfields and harbours, increasing its offensive so that the wisdom of retaining surface ships and the 10th Submarine Flotilla at Malta was daily becoming more doubtful.

Cunningham was not the man to stand idle, however adverse the balance. When two Italian convoys were reported on March 9th, 200 miles from Tripoli, one outward bound, the other homeward, he despatched Vian's cruiser squadron, the *Naiad, Dido,* and *Euryalus* with nine destroyers from Alexandria, early on March 10th, to intercept. The opportunity was also taken to get the cruiser *Cleopatra,* (a new ship of the *Dido* class which had just come out from England), out of Malta, together with the destroyer *Kingston.* Disaster struck again on March 11th, after a day of heavy air attacks, when Vian's flagship the *Naiad* was torpedoed by *U–565,* 50 miles north of the African shore between Mersa Matruh and Sollum, and his force failed to intercept either of the Italian convoys. The *Naiad* sank in 20 minutes; but by good fortune, Vian and his Flag Captain, Guy Grantham, were both saved. They were able to transfer within the next day or two, to the newly arrived *Cleopatra* at Alexandria and Vian then hoisted his flag in his new flagship, and took Grantham with him as his Flag Captain and Chief Staff Officer. The two men made a wonderfully strong combination which must have been largely responsible for the success of the defiant action which was shortly to take place in the Gulf of Sirte.

CHAPTER THREE

Dramatis Personae

Vian was not the easiest of commanders to satisfy. 'Not the chap to hand out the chocolate' as the sailor would express it. It is therefore worth calling attention to his opinion of Grantham as written in *Action This Day,* his autobiography. "It is difficult" he says, "to write a description which would do Grantham justice. Admiral Cunningham describes him as 'that most brilliant and very capable officer'; one could add that he is, and always has been, a very perfect knight, without fear and without reproach." Vian also refers to the selfless efforts of Grantham after finding that it was quite impossible to save his mortally wounded *Naiad.* "Just at the end" Vian writes, "when the last of us were about to take the plunge, I noticed that Grantham was without a lifebelt. I next saw him in the water ferrying two men, beltless non-swimmers, to a raft some distance away: he helped others afterwards, making no attempt to board a raft himself, for they were over-crowded. He was picked up at the end of his tether, completely exhausted, about half an hour later."

Whilst making special reference to Grantham, who after the war rose to the rank of full admiral and also became Governor of Malta, having previously served as Commander-in-Chief, Mediterranean, traditionally one of the most sought after appointments in the Royal Navy, it would be inequitable not to make reference to others of Vian's 'Band of Brothers'. They were a battle-hardened group intent only on the destruction of Axis forces and supplies, and ready to follow Vian to the limit of their ability, despite the continuing possibility of meeting heavy Italian ships, which — on paper at any rate — were materially superior. And let it be remembered that Cunningham was now without aircraft carrier, battleship, or heavy cruiser with which to oppose the Italians should they put to sea.

Though Vian's cruisers were small, they possessed a modern armament of ten 5.25in dual purpose guns, suitable for either a surface action or anti-aircraft fire. They were also fast, and when skilfully and aggressively handled, especially in concentration, could prove more than a match for enemy bombers. The *Cleopatra* was fortunate in having a captain who had already served in two of this class, first in the *Phoebe* which had done splendid work in evacuating the army from Crete, and more recently in the *Naiad*. The *Dido* was of the same class, and her captain, Captain H. W. U. McCall, also had seen much active service in her, including the battle for Crete, where she had received a bomb hit which destroyed B turret necessitating some months of repair in an American yard.

On return of the 15th Cruiser Squadron to Alexandria after the loss of the *Naiad* on March 11th, McCall, as the next senior officer after Vian, had been ordered by Admiral Cunningham to bomb a granary in Rhodes in two days' time. "You needn't worry" Cunningham said, with reference to McCall's concern for Vian. "We are feeding him up on all the stout he can take, and he will be all right. But it's not very nice for you to see your flagship sunk like that. And the answer is a bit of offensive action."

Cunningham was not one to permit much respite. He drove the officers and men of his fleet as he drove himself, and felt much frustrated at a situation which now confined him to his operational and administration headquarters at Alexandria. Such was the confidence he had instilled in the previous two years that the feeling in the fleet had always been: 'if Cunningham is with us, it will be all right'.

So in the early hours of March 15th, McCall with the *Dido, Euryalus,* and six destroyers under his command carried out the bombardment at Rhodes. It was not particularly effectual, but as Captain E. W. Bush of the *Euryalus* writes, "It was good sense to keep us busy with no time to dwell upon the loss of *Naiad*". Bush was another dedicated and efficient officer. On return to Alexandria after the bombardment, he noticed that the *SS Clan Campbell* was back alongside, bomb damage repaired, and again loading stores. This was the ship that had survived the recent abortive attempt to send supplies to Malta, when the two other merchantmen had been sunk. It seemed certain that a further effort was to be made, and indeed co-ordination had already been arranged by Cunningham with the Army and Air Commanders-in-Chief for a combined effort. The Army's long range desert group was to make a diversionary raid on airfields behind the enemy lines at a strategic moment, and the RAF together with the Fleet Air Arm 826 squadron, was to bomb western airfields in Cyrenaica. The RAF Naval Co-operation Group No 201 was to provide air reconnaissance. The idea was to keep enemy aircraft grounded as long as possible during the convoys' passage of 'Bomb Alley'.

It is appropriate here to say a word or two about Vian himself. McCall writes: "In the waters off Alexandria we had rehearsed the tactics to be used should we encounter the Italian Fleet eg divisions acting independently to a large extent with the minimum of signals and using smoke as a cover.

"The aspect that I cannot stress too strongly is that what was achieved was only made possible by team work: a complete and utter trust in our leader, and the knowledge that this was reciprocated by him. Those of us who had served with him for some time could imagine how his mind worked, so that we could conform to his wishes with only the least amount of signalling, knowing exactly how much risk should be taken as each phase of the battle developed."

Grantham writes: "Vian had all the commanding officers of HM ships and the merchant ships to a conference on board before we sailed. He explained to them what he thought would happen and what he intended all ships should do. In the event his forecast was correct, and the only signals he had to make to start the action were 'Enemy in sight' and 'Engage the enemy bearing' . . ."

Bush writes: "My first sight of Vian was on November 11th, 1941 as *Euryalus* was entering Alexandria Harbour. He was standing on the quarterdeck of the *Naiad*. He expected, (almost hoped perhaps), that I should make a pot-mess of picking up the head and stern buoys (he was like that). But little did he know that not only did I enjoy ship-handling but that I had taken the *Devonshire* to the same two buoys in 1939. He was extremely efficient; merciless with the incompetent; and inclined to remain aloof.

"He had the 15th Cruiser Squadron so well trained that it was hardly ever necessary for him to make a signal: the Nelson touch. We all knew what we had to do."

In such capable hands did Cunningham place the responsibility for getting a convoy through to Malta. And this time there must be no failure; whatever the hazard.

The cast then is as follows: for full details see Appendix B.

From Alexandria: *Force B*
15th Cruiser Squadron

Cleopatra	Capt G. Grantham, DSO (Flag of Rear Adm P. L. Vian, DSO)
Dido	Capt H. W. U. McCall
Euryalus	Capt E. W. Bush, DSO, DSC.

14th Destroyer Flotilla

Jervis	(D14)	Capt A. L. Poland, DSO, DSC.
Kipling		Cdr A. St Clair-Ford, DSO.
Kelvin		Cdr J. H. Allison, DSO.
Kingston		Cdr P. Somerville, DSO, DSC.

22nd Destroyer Flotilla

Sikh	(D22)	Capt St J. A. Micklethwait, DSO.
Lively		Lt-Cdr W. F. E. Hussey, DSO, DSC.
Hero		Cdr R. L. Fisher, DSO, OBE.
Havock		Lt-Cdr G. R. G. Watkins, DSC.
Zulu		Cdr H. R. Graham, DSO, DSC.
Hasty		Lt-Cdr N. H. G. Austen

From Alexandria: *Anti-Aircraft Close Escort For Convoy*
A/A Cruiser

Carlisle	Capt D. M. L. Neame, DSO.

5th Destroyer Flotilla
(Hunt Class)

Southwold	Cdr C. T. Jellicoe, DSC.

Beaufort	Lt-Cdr Sir O. G. Roche, Bart.
Dulverton	Lt-Cdr W. N. Petch, OBE.
Hurworth	Lt-Cdr J. T. B. Birch.
Avon Vale	Lt-Cdr P. A. R. Withers, DSC.
Eridge	Lt-Cdr W. F. N. Gregory-Smith, DSC.
Heythrop	Lt-Cdr R. D. Stafford.

From Alexandria: *HM Submarine*
Proteus   Lt-Cdr P. S. Francis

From Malta: *Force K (remnant)*

Penelope	(light cruiser)	Capt A. D. Nicholl, DSO.
Legion	(destroyer)	Cdr R. F. Jessel

From Malta: *HM Submarines*

Unbeaten	Lt-Cdr E. A. Woodward, DSO.
P34	Lt P. R. Harrison, DSC.
Upholder	Lt-Cdr M. D. Wanklyn, VC, DSO.
P36	Lt H. N. Edmunds, DSC.

The destroyers *Kipling, Kelvin,* and *Kingston,* of the 14th Destroyer Flotilla had all served at the Battle for Crete with their respective commanding officers, and the *Jervis* had been at both Crete and the Battle of Matapan. Poland, the new D14, had until recently been Senior Naval Officer of the Inshore Squadron operating off the North African coast, with his headquarters on shore at Tobruk or Mersa Matruh, and had therefore seen as much of the war as most, especially from the small ship point of view.

In the 22nd Destroyer Flotilla, *Hasty* and *Havock* had served both at Matapan and at Crete, the *Havock,* who distinguished herself by sinking the Italian destroyer *Carducci* at Matapan, having had her present commanding officer Watkins at both battles.

In the case of the *Hero,* the captain having gone sick, Fisher "fed-up with being tied to a non-combatant office" asked if he could go in temporary command "for a breath of sea air". He joined late the same evening having missed the briefing conference.

Micklethwait, D22, writes "I had not been long on the

30

station, so did not know my team as well as I did by the time the whole of the 22nd Destroyer Flotilla was sunk in September that year".

It is worth commenting on the segregation of the anti-aircraft section for the close escort duties, a group which distinguished itself in fighting off air attacks. One of the greatest problems in handling general purpose weapons when under attack by air and from surface vessels, was the quick decision as to which target was the most important to engage, especially because switching from one to another involved momentary delay. "Never before" writes McCall, "had we to switch so frequently from surface to anti-aircraft fire".

Finally a word on the convoy itself which was to consist of four fast vessels: the naval supply ship *Breconshire* (10,000 tons), capable of carrying 5,000 tons of oil; and the three merchantmen *Clan Campbell* (7,500 tons), *Pampas* (5,500 tons), and the Norwegian *Talabot* (7,000 tons). The commodore of the convoy was the captain of the *Breconshire,* Captain C. A. G. Hutchinson, DSO, OBE, who had built a wonderful record of service for this fine ship. Cunningham described him as "a fine seaman and stern disciplinarian who inspired his ship's company".

So much then for the British cast. What of the rival cast, as yet unknown to Cunningham or to anyone else. It remained to be seen. Certain it was that that fine seaman Admiral Angelo Iachino, the Italian commander in chief, would be at sea, if he had his will. Nevertheless there was a growing shortage of oil fuel in Italy, and also the national policy was to keep its fleet in being, which really meant keeping ships in a harbour safe from enemy attack; and above all to avoid night action.

Although Cunningham had sunk three of Iachino's heavy cruisers and two destroyers at Matapan, and had slowed down Iachino's flagship the new battleship *Vittorio Veneto,* he had during the night been denied, by Iachino's skilful manoeuvring, the satisfaction of intercepting and claiming the battleship.

Iachino had been Italian naval attache in London 1931–1934, and in his own navy had become an outstanding expert in gunnery. We shall hear more of him later.

CHAPTER FOUR

The Plan

The reader's understanding of the problems underlying the safe conduct of convoy MW 10 to Malta from Alexandria, will be much assisted by reference to Map 3.

The approximately 900 mile journey from Alexandria to Malta can be divided roughly into three parts of 300 miles each. If the convoy could achieve a speed a little in excess of 12 knots, the passage could be conveniently divided into three periods of 24 hours each. In theory then, all being well, the convoy would leave Alexandria at daylight on D day, Friday, March 20th, and arrive off Malta, after three days, at daylight on D+3, Monday, March 23rd. The early setting new moon would give only a minimum of illumination at night, and the hours of darkness on all three days would be almost equal to the hours of daylight, because of the spring equinox.

The major hazards would presumably occur during daylight hours, consisting of evening air reconnaissance and air torpedo and bombing attacks on all three days, March 20th, 21st, and 22nd: D, D+1 and D+2. These might be supplemented by the proximity of Italian heavy ships during daylight on D+2, Sunday, March 22nd. The route would necessarily pass through 'Bomb Alley' between enemy airfields in Crete and Cyrenaica. Fighter cover would be provided by the RAF during the daylight period of the first two days, March 20th and 21st, and it was hoped that diversionary activities by the Army's long-range desert group on enemy airfields would draw off some of the enemy aircraft which would otherwise be expected. It was almost certain that the convoy would be without fighter cover throughout daylight of D+2, since the convoy would, by dawn Sunday March 22nd, be at the limit of the radius of action of British fighters. Once past the bulge of Cyrenaica the convoy would have to keep fairly well to the

HMS *Naiad* Vian's flagship at 1st Battle of Sirte: Sunk by
U-boat off Alexandria 11.3.42 [*IWM*

Above: Convoy MW 10 March 1942, Alexandria to Malta: *Pampas*
(nearest); Norwegian *Talabot* (in middle distance); escorts beyond
[*Grover*

Below: Cleopatra right. (Vian's flag 15.3.42; Capt Grantham) and left,
Euryalus (Bush), engaged with Italian heavy cruisers 22.3.42 [*Grover*

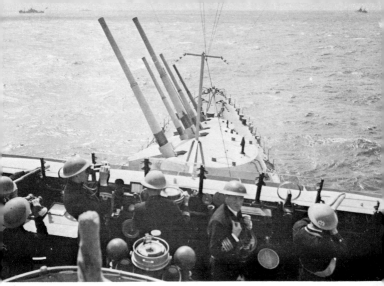

Above: View from *Euryalus's* bridge, ready for air attack; l to r (distance) *Breconshire, Penelope, Cleopatra;* destroyers on horizon [*IWM*

Below: Enemy in sight 22.3.42. *Cleopatra* seen from *Euryalus.* Note the high angle fire from *Cleopatra's* after turrets. [*IWM*

Above: 'Make Smoke', 'Open Fire': *Cleopatra* leads *Euryalus* to the northward [*IWM*

Below: 'Repel Aircraft': Italian S79 (right centre) one minute before crashing into the sea. [*IWM*

Above: Penelope (Nicholl) following *Dido* (McCall) 2nd division in support of the 4th division *(Cleopatra)* and *Euryalus* [*Grover*

Below: 3rd division, *Zulu* (Graham) and hidden in smoke *Hasty* (Austen), on *Dido's* port beam [*Grover*

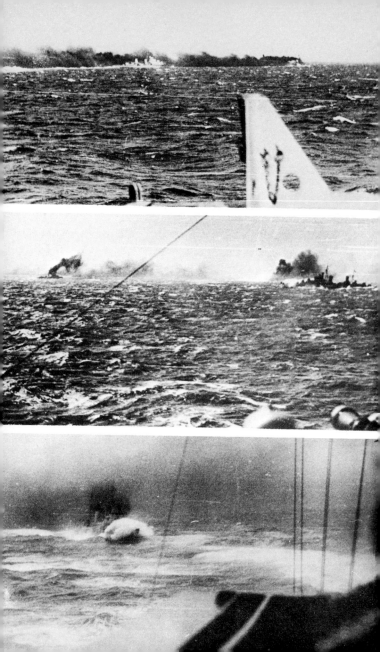

Above: Kipling (St Clair-Ford) breaking through smoke screen in 1st division torpedo attack on the Italian battleship *Littorio [IWM*

Top left: 3rd division later, *Zulu* and *Hasty,* as seen from *Dido [Grover*

Middle left: Hasty left, *Cleopatra* right, returning from search to the east, seen from *Dido.* Note 5th division's smoke screen on horizon [*Grover*

Bottom left: Shipping a large sea: *Penelope* following *Dido:* both of 2nd division [*Grover*

Left: In the *Dido* the captain's leading steward serves tea on the bridge during a lull [*Grover*

Below left: Captain Henry McCall on *Dido's* bridge during a lull: helmets have been shed, but Mae Wests are retained [*Grover*

Above right: HMS *Dido* (severely damaged at Crete 29.5.41) fought at Sirte 22.3.42 [*IWM*

Below right: Emerging from the smoke: a tense moment on *Dido's* bridge [*Grover*

Above: HMS *Cleopatra* destined for Alexandria from UK, entering Grand Harbour, Malta, Feb 1942 for repairs after Stuka attack off Malta. Later to hoist Vian's flag 15.3.42 [*IWM*

Below: l to r Capt Grantham, Rear Adm Vian, Rear Adm Norman, Mr R. G. Casey, (Minister of State, Middle East), on *Cleopatra's* quarterdeck at Alexandria 1942 [*IWM*

Above: Rear Adm St J. A. Micklethwait; Capt. D22 at Sirte in the *Sikh,* and leader of the 5th division 22.3.42

Below: Tribal class: HMS *Sikh* (Micklethwaite); 22nd Destroyer Flotilla Leader and leader of 5th division, 22.3.42. Lost 14.9.42 [*IWM*

Above: L class: HMS *Lively* (Hussey); 22nd DF and 5th division, 22.3.42. Lost 11.5.42 [*IWM*

Top: H class: HMS *Hero* (Fisher); 22nd DF and 5th division 22.3.42. Survived World War II [*IWM*

Above left: H class: HMS *Havock* (Watkins); 22nd DF and 5th division, 22.3.42. Lost 6.4.42.

Left: Commander H. R. Graham, 3rd division leader in *Zulu* 22.3.42 (seen here as captain of the *Pursuer*) [*IWM*

Right: H class: HMS *Hasty* (Austen); 3rd division 22.3.42. Lost 15.6.42 [*IWM*

Above left: Arethusa class: HMS *Penelope* (Nicholl) of Force K, Malta; entering Grand Harbour 5.12.41; 2nd division with *Dido* 22.3.42. Lost 18.2.44 [*IWM*

Below left: Dido class: HMS *Euryalus* (Bush) passing through Suez Canal Nov 1941 for service in the Med: She survived World War II [*IWM*

Below: Penelope's Captain A. D. Nicholl and Commander J. Grant [*IWM*

Above: Tribal class: HMS *Zulu* (Graham); 3rd division 22.3.42. Lost 14.9.42 [*IWM*

Below: Italian battleship *Littorio* (flag of the Italian C-in-C Adm Iachino 22.3.42) Scrapped at La Spezia [*IWM*

south, so as to increase the distance from Italian surface forces trying to intercept. This could not, however, be done without increasing the distance to be covered to reach Malta, thereby dangerously delaying the plan to arrive by dawn of D+3, Monday, March 23rd. Although British fighters would not be able to reach the region of the convoy during the period of daylight on Sunday March 22nd, it was hoped to provide long range British bombers for an air striking force in the event of any Italian surface force or convoy being reported at sea.

In order to gain early information of the movements of Italian ships, three British submarines *P36, Proteus,* and *Upholder* were sent off to patrol the approaches to Taranto, while the *Unbeaten* and *P34* were to patrol the Straits of Messina. See Map 7.

The remnants of Force K, the cruiser *Penelope* and the destroyer *Legion* were to leave Malta and proceed eastward in time to rendezvous with Vian's force and the convoy at daylight D+2, Sunday, March 22nd.

A further group taking part in the plan was Force H from Gibraltar which hoped to fly in 16 Spitfires to Malta on March 21st, and thus draw off some of the aircraft of Fliegerkorps II.

A copy of Vian's intentions was sent by air to the *Penelope* at Malta, but failed to reach Captain Nicholl before his ship sailed after dark on March 21st for the rendezvous with Vian next morning. Nicholl was, however, to be left in no doubt as to what was expected of him once he joined Force B.

Vian's plan was to organise his whole force so that a certain disposition could be quickly assumed if and when enemy surface forces were sighted. The principle was that speed and initiative displayed by the small ships of the various divisions of his force would harass and threaten a materially superior enemy by repeated assaults and withdrawals, and thus prevent them from destroying the convoy. Such tactics could be greatly assisted by the liberal use of smoke screens which would not only prevent the enemy warships from sighting the convoy, but would also conceal the imminence of short range gunfire action and, what was of even greater concern for the enemy, torpedo attacks.

The principle of harassing a battleship with repeated assault and withdrawal by cruisers, had been most gallantly and successfully demonstrated by Admiral Sir Henry Harwood at the battle of the River Plate, when the German pocket battleship *Graf Spee* had had to retire to Montevideo in December 1939. Such tactics were not new, for they had been suggested by Admiral Kempenfelt to the First Lord of the Admiralty, Sir Charles Middleton, (later Lord Barham) in July 1779. "Much depends on this fleet" he had said; "tis an inferior against a superior fleet; therefore the greatest skill and address is requisite to counteract the designs of the enemy, to watch and seize the favourable opportunity for action . . . to hover near the enemy, keep him at bay, and prevent his attempting to execute anything but at risk and hazard . . . and oblige them to think of nothing but being on their guard".*

Vian's plan, in the event of sighting the enemy, was to have:

(a) a striking force to attack and harass the enemy warships

(b) a special smoke-laying division to lay smoke across the wake of the convoy

(c) a close anti-aircraft escort for the convoy.

This disposition for surface action, to be assumed in place of the normal cruising disposition designed to meet air attack, was to be taken up with the least possible delay, the plan being as follows. In the event *Legion* spent most of the time with the *Jervis* division and not with *Dido*.

(a) *Striking Force Divisions*
   1st (Under Capt Poland, D14) *Jervis, Kipling, Kelvin, Kingston*.
   2nd (Under Capt McCall) *Dido, Penelope, Legion*.
   3rd (Under Cdr Graham) *Zulu, Hasty*.
   4th (Under R-Adm Vian) *Cleopatra, Euryalus*.
   5th (Under Capt Micklethwaite, D22) *Sikh, Lively, Hero, Havock*.
(b) *Smoke-laying Division*
   6th (Under Capt Neame) *Carlisle, Avon Vale*.
(c) *Close Escort*

*The Barham Papers, Navy Records Society, Vol 1 p292.

7th   (Under Cdr Jellicoe) *Southwold, Beaufort, Dulverton, Hurworth, Eridge, Heythrop.*

The Commander-in-Chief's orders covered all contingencies. One of the biggest problems for all sorties to the central Mediterranean was the supply of ammunition and fuel, and this particularly applied to the small Hunt class destroyers; see Appendix J. Since Malta could spare neither fuel nor ammunition, the duration of a sortie was restricted by the limitations imposed by a ship's own capacity. The Hunts were therefore sent off from Alexandria the night before the convoy was due to sail from Alexandria. They were to carry out an anti-submarine search ahead of Vian's force as far as Tobruk, (still in British hands), and then refuel at Tobruk prior to joining Vian on the morning of D+1, Saturday March 21st, by which time the convoy would have completed a third of its journey. By daylight the next morning Vian's force would have been joined by Force K. He was then to proceed at full strength during this critical day of uncertainty, until dark, steering well to the southward of the direct course for Malta. As soon as it was dark on that Sunday, March 22nd, Vian was to detach the convoy for Malta, together with the anti-aircraft cruiser *Carlisle* and the Hunts, with the object of their reaching Malta before daylight the next morning. Vian himself was to turn back for Alexandria with his 15th Cruiser Squadron and the Fleet destroyers.

Admiral Cunningham reckoned on intervention by the Italian fleet during daylight of Sunday, March 22nd. "Should this occur" his orders ran, "it is my general intention that the enemy should, if possible, be evaded until darkness, after which the convoy should be sent on to Malta with the destroyer escort, being dispersed if considered advisable, and the enemy brought to action by Force B. The convoy should only be turned back if it is evident that the enemy will otherwise intercept in daylight and east of longitude 18° E." The presumption was that if the convoy was west of longitude 18° E by daylight, there would be a good chance of receiving fighter protection, since the convoy would then be less than 200 miles from Malta. Unfortunately, on the day in question

Malta airfields were to be subjected to very heavy air attack.

With a typical Nelson touch, Vian dined his captains in the *Cleopatra* the night before sailing from Alexandria.

CHAPTER FIVE

Curtain Up

In accordance with the plan, the seven Hunt class destroyers sailed from Alexandria during the night before D day to carry out an anti-submarine search between Alexandria and Tobruk. This operation continued during daylight hours of Friday, March 20th, but was soon attended by misfortune of an ironic character, for the *Heythrop* was herself torpedoed by a submarine on that day. She sank whilst on her way to Tobruk in tow. The remaining six Hunts oiled at Tobruk, but one of these got her propeller fouled and was unable to leave Tobruk with the other five to join the convoy.

Meanwhile the convoy, known as MW 10, consisting of the *Breconshire* and the three merchant ships *Clan Campbell, Pampas,* and *Talabot,* had sailed from Alexandria on the morning of Friday, March 20th, together with the anti-aircraft cruiser *Carlisle* and six Fleet destroyers.

The same evening after dark, Vian sailed from Alexandria with the 15th Cruiser Squadron accompanied by four Fleet destroyers, and closed the convoy on the forenoon of March 21st, some 70 miles north of Tobruk. By this time the five Hunts had also joined from Tobruk, and the sixth, which had suffered a delay in clearing her propeller, was also able to join on the evening of March 21st. Passage through 'Bomb Alley' was attended by relays of fighter aircraft overhead and all was going according to plan, except that the *Clan Campbell* had difficulty in keeping up the 12 knots that had been presumed. The captain of the *Breconshire* wrote: "*Clan Campbell* could not go more than about 9 knots whereas she should have been good for 12 knots. We were, therefore, behind time all the way. This had a tremendous influence on the outcome of the operation".

In spite of the mishaps mentioned, the operation was going

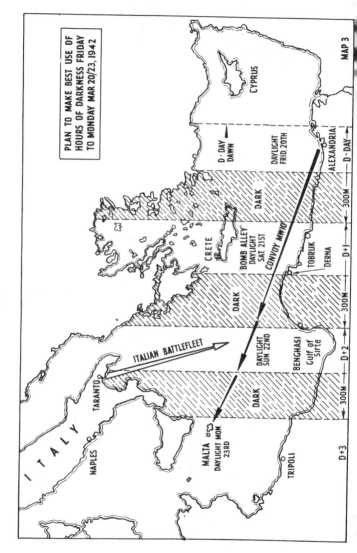

PLAN TO MAKE BEST USE OF
HOURS OF DARKNESS FRIDAY
TO MONDAY MAR 20/23, 1942

MAP 3

CYPRUS

ITALY

NAPLES

TARANTO

ITALIAN BATTLEFLEET

CRETE

BOMB ALLEY
DAYLIGHT
SAT. 21ST
CONVOY MWID?

DARK

DARK

DAYLIGHT
SUN 22ND

Gulf of
Sirte

BENGHASI

DERNA

TOBRUK

ALEXANDRIA

D - DAY DAWN

DAYLIGHT
FRID. 20TH

D - DAY

300M

DARK

300M

D+1

300M

D+2

300M

DARK

D+3

MALTA
DAYLIGHT MON.
23RD

TRIPOLI

38

well, particularly as the diversionary activities planned for the Army were pinning down Axis aircraft very successfully, and the RAF and FAA attacks on Axis airfields kept the enemy fully occupied. "Consequently" says an Italian report, "the Axis air forces in North Africa did not carry out any reconnaissance flights at sea". It is also evident that the passage eastward of British aircraft carriers to the south of the Balearic Islands, taking Spitfires within flying distance of Malta, occupied the attention of other Axis reconnaissance planes. Number 826 Fleet Air Arm Squadron which had performed so well with their Swordfish and Albacores at the battle of Matapan, and were now based ashore, worked with the RAF in bombing targets at Derna on the nights of D day and D+1.

"All the British measures adopted to prevent the convoy from being sighted by our air reconnaissance were successful" writes Bragadin, giving the Axis viewpoint in *The Italian Navy in World War II*. Nevertheless Vian's force was seen and reported at 17.00 on the evening of D+1 by German Ju 52 transport aircraft flying from Cyrenaica to Crete. And three quarters of an hour later his presence was reported by the Italian submarine *Onice*. Vian was scarcely surprised therefore upon intercepting a signal made by British submarine *P36* early the next morning D+2, to learn that heavy Italian ships had left Taranto at 01.00 Sunday, March 22nd. *P36* reported the course and speed of these ships as 150°, 23 knots, but was unable to give the number and class of the ships.

Vian continued on course for his rendezvous with *Penelope* and *Legion,* both of whom joined him at 08.00 in position 34° 10'N, 19° 30'E, on this critical day, Sunday, March 22nd.

"As we met the formation" writes Nicholl the captain of the *Penelope,* "on the morning of the 22nd, the *Penelope* passed close to the *Cleopatra* and I could see Vian on the bridge greeting me by making a large V sign with his arms." Vian was unaware that the *Penelope* and *Legion* had not received a copy of his orders.

Vian still had fighter cover, but the fighters were now almost at the limiting radius of action, and at 09.00 the last fighter patrol would have to leave the convoy to return to Egypt. Air attacks could be expected at any moment after that. Vian's force was now complete, and the convoy well on its way to Malta, having passed through 'Bomb Alley' without attack. The convoy was at the moment making good about 11½ knots, but still had 75 miles to go to reach the hoped-for, albeit doubtful, security of longitude 18° E. This should take about 6½ hours, all being well, which indicated that they ought to arrive at this critical meridian at about 14.30. If they altered course substantially to southward of their westerly course, it would take longer and could mean a later interception by the Italian fleet. This, however, would lengthen the journey for the convoy, and delay the possibility of obtaining fighter cover from Malta. On the other hand the later the interception by the Italian ships, the shorter would be the period before darkness brought its merciful cover.

The weather was fair on this Sunday morning, and the visibility good, but both were rapidly deteriorating. There was a fresh and increasing south-easterly wind. The sea was rough with a moderate swell, and was hourly getting worse. Wind, visibility, and sea would prove to be vital factors, both in fighting off air attacks and in engaging enemy ships in a surface action.

Vian's main query was the position and progress of the heavy Italian ships which had been reported early that morning. If he assumed for them a likely 'speed made good' of 28 knots, (all Italian ships were fast), they could cover a distance of 360 miles in 13 hours. This suggested that they would intercept his direct track for Malta (now bearing 293° ie west-north-west) at about 14.00 that afternoon. On the other hand, the Italians might well be slowed down because of increasing head winds and a rising sea which must affect in particular any destroyers in company as a screen for the heavy ships. A more likely time of interception was therefore nearer 16.00 than 14.00.

Vian had been steering 270° for the rendezvous and now at 08.00 altered a point to the south of west, to steer 250°. The convoy might still elude the Italian ships by passing well ahead of them, and then dash on through the night for Malta.

At 09.30, just half an hour after the last fighter patrol had left Vian's force, air attacks began. These were to continue, with only brief respite but with increasing intensity, for the rest of the day until dark. At first there were high-level bombers, torpedo bombers, and shadowers. The convoy was protected at this stage by two screens: an outer anti-submarine screen provided by the Fleet destroyers two miles ahead, and an inner anti-aircraft screen provided by the cruisers and the Hunt class destroyers.

Capt Nicholl of the *Penelope* described the torpedo bomber attacks by Italian S79 aircraft as "futile" because of the long range at which torpedoes were dropped.

Capt Hutchison of the *Breconshire* writes: "During that afternoon and evening we had no less than 16 bombing attacks from the Luftwaffe and 3 torpedo bombing attacks. I had opened out the convoy so that each ship could safely take avoiding action independently: whilst during the torpedo bombing attacks I manoeuvred the convoy as a whole to avoid the torpedoes; no ship was hit or even damaged by near misses". With the double screen round the convoy the anti-aircraft fire from the entire force proved a sufficient deterrent. Nevertheless with the possibility of the arrival of Italian ships from the northward in the afternoon, Vian decided to assume his disposition for surface action. This he did at 12.30, determined in his own mind that the convoy should go through. In accordance with his plan, the *Carlisle* and *Avon Vale* prepared instantly to lay a smoke screen to prevent enemy ships sighting the convoy. The Hunts were to form a close escort round the convoy and to continue in company with it. The five divisions of the striking force were to be ready for a surface engagement to the northward as soon as the enemy ships appeared, or, if Vian decided against an immediate close engagement, to resort to the diversionary tactics previously practised, whereby the concentrated divisions would lay smoke screens at right angles to the bearing of the enemy, and reverse course in time to attack with torpedoes as the enemy reached the smoke. It was known that the Italians were wary of entering smoke.

Vian's only report of enemy ships had come from submarine *P36*. Air reconnaissance from Malta had been frustrated both by the bad weather and by heavy bombing. But all was ready, and the seemingly long wait now began. Perhaps the Italian ships would not arrive before nightfall.

CHAPTER SIX

Enemy in Sight

Vian's force had assumed its special disposition at 12.30. He was not long to be kept in suspense concerning enemy ships, for at 13.30 an enemy float-plane, obviously from a warship, dropped a string of bright red flares over the convoy to indicate the line of advance. Meanwhile the bombing of the convoy became heavier as Ju 88s attacked.

Captain Bush of the *Euryalus* had excellent eyesight and was determined that his ship should have the distinction of first sighting the enemy ships. It was another *Euryalus*, a frigate captained by Blackwood, that on the eve of Trafalgar, had first sighted the combined French and Spanish fleets emerging from Cadiz in 1805.

At 14.10 Bush sighted and reported smoke on his horizon bearing 350°. He followed this at 14.17 with a report of "Three ships bearing 350°!" Up went the signal flags in *Euryalus*, closely followed by a similar message from the destroyer *Legion*. "But we were definitely first" writes Bush in *Bless Our Ship*.

This was immediately followed by Vian's pre-discussed executive signal, for divisions to concentrate in readiness for a surface action and to make smoke. He led off to the north, leaving the convoy steering a new course to the south-west. The sighting of enemy ships had happened somewhat earlier than expected but he was ready.

At 14.27 *Euryalus* reported four ships bearing 015°, *Legion* at the same time reported one ship bearing 010°, distant 12 miles. "As the Italian masts came in sight" wrote Vian "they were taken for those of battleships, and our main force moved to meet them, leaving *Carlisle* and the six Hunts as sole protectors of the heavily-bombed convoy".

It was clear to Vian that since his force was unable to oil at

Malta, it could not long be entangled in operations so far to the westward of Alexandria. Nor could the convoy afford to continue too far to the south-westward when every hour's delay decreased the chances of their reaching Malta before daylight and of their being bombed on the morrow. The enemy therefore must be driven off before dark.

Ship identification requires special study, but it was a well known fact that many of the Italian cruisers employed in World War II, very much resembled battleships; and in like manner some of their larger destroyers were often mistaken for cruisers. As the enemy ships closed and their details were more clearly visible, it became evident that the group consisted of two heavy cruisers, one light cruiser, and four destroyers. Unknown to Vian this was a squadron under Admiral Parona, that had left Messina, unreported, at 01.00 that day at about the same time that the battleship *Littorio* (unspecified at that time) had been reported leaving Taranto. The heavy cruisers were the *Gorizia* and *Trento* capable of 30 knots or more, and each carrying eight 8in guns (compared with the *Dido* class ten 5.25in guns). The light cruiser was the *Bande Nere* with a top speed well in excess of 30 knots and carrying eight 6in guns. It was intended that this squadron should link with the battleship *Littorio* and four destroyers and come under the orders of the commander-in-chief, Admiral Iachino, flying his flag in the *Littorio*.

Commander Bragadin says, "Because of the situation at Malta, no enemy aircraft sighted the Italian ships during the entire mission, and the Italian formation proceeded along on the morning of the 22nd, certain that the convoy would be taken by surprise".

However, because of the difficulty that the Italian destroyers were having, steaming head on to the developing south-easterly gale, "the whole Italian formation" says Bragadin, "could proceed at no more than 22 knots, thus postponing ultimate contact ... In addition, the destroyer *Grecale* had an engine breakdown and had to turn back to Taranto, leaving the *Littorio* with an escort of only three destroyers".

As Vian's striking force drew off to the north, and away from the convoy, his ships formed divisions in line ahead, as instructed in the operation orders: ie all except *Penelope* and *Legion* who had no orders.

"At 14.30" writes Nicholl, captain of the *Penelope*, "the *Euryalus* sighted smoke to the north-eastward and hoisted the signal 'Enemy in Sight'. Vian at once made 'Carry out pre-arranged plan'.

"The convoy and all the ships of the escort then began moving in various directions at high speed. I, unfortunately, had no knowledge of any pre-arranged plan; no previous orders of any kind had reached the *Penelope*. However there is a well-tried course of action I had learned in my time in destroyers; 'When in doubt, follow father'. So I tacked on to Vian's cruisers, and *Legion* joined the nearest destroyer division. Though I had no instructions, I had no difficulty in sensing what Vian wanted the cruisers to do.

"McCall in the *Dido*, however, knew that the *Penelope* should have been astern of him. He had also noticed that the *Penelope*, though conforming to the movements of the other cruisers, was acting in a somewhat independent way. Vian led us towards the enemy at high speed and all the cruisers made smoke. The smoke, carried by a rising south-easterly wind, was lying perfectly. There was a long-range gun battle and a number of shell splashes fell close to the *Penelope*. But the enemy soon turned away and Vian at once led us back to the convoy.

"As soon as we were clear of the smoke McCall signalled 'What is seniority of captain?' 'June 1939' I replied. 'Take station astern' he signalled at once. Well, now I knew the *Penelope's* position in the cruisers' battle formation. It was a great help."

At 14.33 divisions turned east to lay smoke, an operation most effectively assisted by the freshening south-easterly wind. "As soon as our ships were sighted by the enemy", stated an Italian report, "he spread a smoke cloud which after only 40 seconds completely covered the convoy and blotted out a large area of the surrounding sea".

When first seen, the Italian cruisers and destroyers appeared to be steaming south-west towards the convoy in a loose line abreast. Their distance was then about 14 miles but they were closing rapidly, until at 14.45 they turned together to

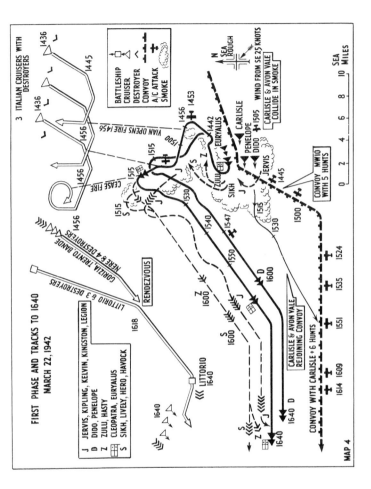

FIRST PHASE AND TRACKS TO 1640
MARCH 22, 1942

J   JERVIS, KIPLING, KELVIN, KINGSTON, LEGION
D   DIDO, PENELOPE
Z   ZULU, HASTY
    CLEOPATRA, EURYALUS
S   SIKH, LIVELY, HERO, HAVOCK

BATTLESHIP
CRUISER
DESTROYER
CONVOY
A/C ATTACK
SMOKE

3 ITALIAN CRUISERS WITH DESTROYERS

1436
1445
1436
1456
1456
1456

VIAN OPENS FIRE 1456
1500
1515
CEASE FIRE
1515
1515
1515
1530

1456
1436

1456
LITTORIO TRENTO BANDE
NERE & 4 DESTROYERS
LITTORIO & 3 DESTROYERS
CONZIA
RENDEZVOUS
1618
LITTORIO
1640
1640
1600
1600
1600
1600
1640 D
1640 S Z
1640

1453
1442
1515
EURYALUS
CARLISLE
PENELOPE
DIDO
1505
CARLISLE & AVON VALE
COLLIDE IN SMOKE

WIND FROM SE 25 KNOTS
SEA ROUGH
N
WIND

ZULU
SIKH
J
S
Z
J
S
JERVIS
1445
1500
1530
1547
1550
1600 D

CONVOY MW10 WITH 5 HUNTS

CARLISLE & AVON VALE
REJOINING CONVOY

1524   1535   1551   1609   1614

CONVOY WITH CARLISLE + 6 HUNTS

MAP 4

SEA MILES
0   2   4   6   8   10

starboard to steer west-south-west for a few minutes and then to west-north-west, so as to bring guns to bear, while beam on to Vian's striking force.

Having steamed east for some minutes to make smoke, Vian was able to see at 14.42 that he was opposed by heavy cruisers and not battleships. He now led again with the *Cleopatra* and *Euryalus* towards the Italians to close the range, and at 14.56 when the range had fallen to 10 miles, began a concentrated shoot on the nearest cruiser: see Map 4.

It is interesting to record a personal description by Commander Fisher, then captain of the *Hero*, who was following *Lively* in the *Sikh* division led by Captain Micklethwait. "I only joined *Hero* late and missed the briefing conference" says Fisher. "I don't remember anything of the first day or two until the moment when smoke having been sighted to the north, the Fleet destroyers extricated themselves at high speed from their convoy screening stations, and some of them passing through the convoy, formed on their leaders and sped away to do battle. A dramatic moment.

"I was fully occupied throughout the action, in hanging on to our next ahead [*Lively*] in thick smoke without ramming her. I never had the opportunity to look at a plot, and had only the haziest idea where any other formations were. A few big splashes fell near us once or twice, and *Havock* I think, next astern, was hit, but not very badly.

"I can remember once coming out of smoke for a minute or two amid a continuous roar of gunfire and seeing the convoy some miles away being attacked by aircraft, the whole sky above it being pock-marked by the black bursts of a tremendous barrage being put up by the Hunt class destroyers who had remained with it."

Commander St Clair-Ford who was in command of the *Kipling* presents a similar picture of this particular phase as seen from the *Jervis* division led by Poland, and which with the addition of the *Legion* now consisted of five destroyers.

"The report that smoke was sighted to northward" says St Clair-Ford, "made everyone tingle with excitement, for it now seemed certain that enemy surface units were going to have a crack at us. Very shortly afterwards the superstructures of three cruisers were sighted. The excellence of the Admiral's operation orders was now seen. Without any signals, the convoy altered course to the south-westward, the cruisers moved out to close the enemy, making smoke at the same time, whilst the destroyers which had formed up behind their respective divisional leaders simultaneously made extra smoke to cover the retirement of the convoy.

"By this time a strong south-east wind had got up with a rising sea. It was difficult to see what was actually happening, for the whole ocean seemed to be full of the most effective smoke screen through which the cruisers emerged from time to time, and the whole scene of this engagement was also being plastered with enemy shells and the occasional aeroplane bombs.

"Throughout this engagement, the convoy (and also cruisers and destroyers) were being heavily bombed, but the gallant little Hunt class destroyers put up some superb gunfire, and not a single ship in that party was hit, whilst several planes were shot down."

Before concluding this chapter which deals with the preliminary engagement or curtain raiser for the main battle, it is timely to view a little closer the scenes inside one of the destroyers at Sirte, as seen by Lt-Cdr Aylen the Engineer Officer of the *Kelvin* in the *Jervis* division.

"That something was afoot" writes Aylen, "was obvious from the rapid changes in course and disposition of the cruisers, so the order 'make smoke' was no surprise, only an added irritation. It involved cutting off the air and adding a small supply of cold un-atomised oil which made thick black funnel smoke, the screening effectiveness of which was entirely dependent on the wind force, humidity, and strength of purpose of the boilerroom's crew, who knew only too well the potential risk of fire in the uptakes let alone the subsequent loathsome chimney-sweeping in port."

As Vian opened fire at 14.56 at a range of 10 miles in a concentrated shoot at one of the heavy cruisers, the Italians turned abruptly away to the north-west, and later to the northward. The exchange of fire was at extreme range, and although the 6in cruiser *Bande Nere* straddled the *Cleopatra* and *Euryalus*, no hits were scored by either side. By 15.15 the

Italian ships were steaming northward, well out of range.

Because of the interference of their own smoke, few of the British ships were able to sight the Italians. But it was probably the fear of a torpedo attack from out of the smoke that caused Admiral Parona to retire to close his Commander-in-Chief with the cruiser squadron. The Italian explanation was that they wished to decoy the British ships to a confrontation with Iachino.

As the Italian ships withdrew, Vian altered course to rejoin the convoy now steering westward towards Malta.

CHAPTER SEVEN

Vian Rejoins the Convoy

The withdrawal of Admiral Parona's force to the northwards and the ceasefire that immediately followed, took place at 15.15. Vian was still unaware of the fact that the battleship *Littorio* was at sea. Early that morning he had intercepted *P36's* report of unspecified heavy enemy ships leaving Taranto, bound for the south. Upon sighting Parona's cruisers therefore at 14.27 he was not to know that these vessels were anything but the heavy ships previously reported. He had driven them off. And soon after 15.15 he had altered course with his divisions, to steer 235°, to close the convoy now steaming westward (See Map 4).

During the brief engagement between Vian's striking force and the Italian cruisers, there had been attacks by Italian high-level and torpedo bombers, but these had caused no damage. Air attacks on the convoy however had been severe and frequent, but here again no damage had been done, thanks to the good shooting of the *Carlisle* and the Hunt class destroyers. The expenditure of ammunition had, however, been serious. *Carlisle* reported spending one-third of her outfit; but Jellicoe of the *Southwold,* senior officer of the Hunts, had a worse tale and reported "Nine attacks so far: 40 per cent 4in ammunition remaining".

The performance of the Hunts was gratifying, and fully justified their development which had been sponsored by Cunningham in 1938 when he was serving as Deputy Chief of the Naval Staff at the Admiralty. But their small size seriously limited the amount of ammunition they could carry. It had been Cunningham's intention that they should be small in order that reasonable numbers could be produced by the time war broke out. They were adaptable, and fully proved their value.

In Alexandria Cunningham was watching every reported event on a large chart in his war room, experiencing "the mortifying bitterness of sitting behind the scenes with a heavy load of responsibility while others were in action against a vastly superior force of the enemy".

It is interesting to gain a picture of Cunningham, who did not find it easy to sit in an armchair and send ships to sea, fully realizing the hazards and hardships involved. Lt-Col R. B. Moseley, who was the army liaison officer at the Naval Headquarters at Alexandria describes the scene. "One of the most thrilling and memorable events in my life was attending the operations room during the whole of Admiral Vian's escort of a vital convoy to Malta with his light cruisers, when the Italian battleship *Littorio,* heavy cruisers, and escorts, came out to intercept. The excellence of Naval communications meant that Cunningham had his operations table plotted with the movements of both forces, and he received all signals and sightings as they were made. Never once did he interfere though continually making such comments as 'Good boy', 'That is correct'."

At 15.35, 20 minutes after the withdrawal of Parona's force northward, Vian made a signal to the Commander-in-Chief in Alexandria, saying simply 'Enemy driven off'. This was tremendous relief for Cunningham, and so far all was well, but the weather continued to deteriorate. Cunningham sums up the situation in the following words:

"In the heavy sea and the rising wind the destroyers had been fighting their guns in the most difficult conditions, with their gun crews drenched. The ships were washing down forward and aft. Even the bridges and director towers of the cruisers were swept by heavy spray when they steamed to windward."

The *Carlisle,* with the Hunt destroyer *Avon Vale,* had between 14.45 and 15.00, made a good leg to windward in the wake of the convoy, putting up a smoke screen that spread effectively in the right direction towards the enemy, blotting out the convoy from the port quarter right across to the starboard quarter. They received various air attacks that were driven off, and the *Carlisle* had a narrow escape from bombs. As a result of manoeuvring to avoid the bombs, and because of the thick smoke, *Carlisle* came into collision with the *Avon Vale*, but fortunately only minor damage was sustained.

The convoy also received a heavy assault from the air which began at 14.45 and continued at intervals of 10 minutes or more. These assaults were mainly delivered by German Ju 88 bombers, varying in number from three to nine aircraft, some in high-level attacks, others in diving attacks from 9,000 feet. Thanks to the steady shooting of the Hunts and Hutchison's skilful handling of the convoy, no hits were scored by the aircraft. Particular credit was given by Jellicoe of the *Southwold* to the guns' crews on the forecastles of the destroyers, who were fighting their guns though drenched by the heavy seas that swept the decks.

As Vian turned to the south-west soon after 15.15 to join the convoy, the latter was a matter of 15 to 16 miles from him, hidden in clouds of smoke. It was not long, however, before he was aware of the continued heavy air attack on the convoy. "Whilst the striking force was rejoining" he wrote, "the sound of the 4in fire from the Hunts and *Carlisle* was most impressive, resembling continuous pom-pom fire, even though heard at a distance of 8 to 10 miles." The stocks of ammunition were rapidly being consumed. Vian ordered Poland's division the *Jervis, Kipling, Kelvin,* and *Kingston,* now supplemented by the *Legion,* to join the close escort, so as to ease the high consumption of ammunition then being suffered by the Hunts.

In the meantime, Admiral Iachino, unknown to Vian had been steering southward all day, steaming at 28 knots, though only making good something less than 25 knots (See Map 7). His force now consisted of the *Littorio* and three destroyers and was some way astern of Admiral Parona's cruisers. He intended a rendezvous at the appropriate moment.

At 09.55 Admiral Iachino had received an aircraft report which placed a considerable British naval force in position 34° 10'N, 19° 10'E, steering west at 14 knots. The aircraft had mistakenly identified at least one of the ships of the convoy as a battleship, but Iachino was not to know that.

Iachino decided to keep his forces to the westward of the British forces in order to stand a good chance of interception, and to bar the British passage to Malta. Also the nearer to

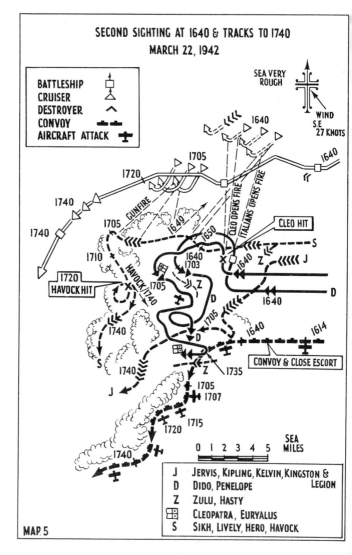

SECOND SIGHTING AT 1640 & TRACKS TO 1740
MARCH 22, 1942

SEA VERY ROUGH

WIND
S.E.
27 KNOTS

BATTLESHIP
CRUISER
DESTROYER
CONVOY
AIRCRAFT ATTACK

1640

1705
1720
1640
1740
1740
1710
1705
GUNFIRE
1649
1650
CLEO OPENS FIRE
ITALIANS OPENS FIRE
CLEO HIT
S
Z
J
1640
1720
HAVOCK HIT
HAVOCK
1740
1640
1703
1705
Z
D
D
1640
1705
1640
1614
1740
S
D
CONVOY & CLOSE ESCORT
1740
J
Z
1735
1705
1707
1720
1715
1740

SEA MILES
0 1 2 3 4 5

J   JERVIS, KIPLING, KELVIN, KINGSTON & LEGION
D   DIDO, PENELOPE
Z   ZULU, HASTY
     CLEOPATRA, EURYALUS
S   SIKH, LIVELY, HERO, HAVOCK

MAP. 5

Sicily he remained, the greater the prospect of Luftwaffe support during daylight. Accordingly he gradually hauled round during the day to the south-westward, altering to 200° at 13.53 for the rendezvous with Parona. At 16.18 he was joined by Parona's cruisers and altered to 200°.

"At 16.18" writes Bragadin, "the *Littorio* joined Parona's Division, but the sea had become very rough, the wind had risen to almost 50 kilometers an hour [27 knots], and a dense mist made the visibility very poor."

Vian had barely joined the convoy and taken station five miles to the north of it at 16.40, when the Italian ships came in sight (see Map 5). This time they bore north-east distant 10 miles, steering head on for Vian. They looked a truly formidable force.

CHAPTER EIGHT

Heavy Ships Reappear

The sighting signal at second contact came first from the *Zulu* at 16.37 reporting "unknown ships". This was followed at 16.40 by one from the *Euryalus*. As the situation developed it became clear that there were two enemy groups, one bearing north some 10 miles away, the other bearing north-east also distant 10 miles (see Map 5).

The first group was in due course identified as two 8in cruisers (actually the *Gorizia* and *Trento*), and a 6in cruiser (the *Bande Nere*); these being accompanied by four destroyers. The second group consisted of the battleship *Littorio* (Iachino's flagship) with three destroyers. Both groups were steaming at high speed to the south-west and were in a good position to intercept the convoy.

As soon as the *Euryalus* report had been received, Vian's striking forces led towards the north, with the exception of the five destroyers of the *Jervis* division under Poland, who held on for some time towards the convoy in accordance with previous orders to lend support to the five Hunts of the close escort.

The Italian account of this confrontation appears to belittle the material superiority of their force, and refers to the fact that the British had five cruisers and 18 destroyers against an Italian force of only one battleship, three cruisers and seven destroyers.

In the event, since the *Carlisle* was fully occupied in fighting off air attacks on the convoy and required the full time assistance of six Hunts, Vian had but four light cruisers and 11 Fleet destroyers available to deal with Iachino's forces. The disparity is evident when it is realised that Vian's total broadside would then be but 5,900 pounds against Iachino's total of 24,000 pounds. And at the moment, five of his Fleet destroyers — those of Poland's division — were committed to the support of the Hunts in the close escort of the convoy to the southward.

Iachino sighted Vian's forces at 16.31 in the now patchy and deteriorating visibility, shortly to be aggravated by the "vast masses of smoke spread by the English vessels." Soon after 16.40 Iachino altered course to 290°. Vian's forces had appeared some 10 miles further west than Iachino had anticipated, and Iachino now had to decide which of the following three possibilities he must select.

First, he could pull away westward to his right, so as to "interpose his ships between Malta and the enemy group, and eventually come round to them from the west". Second, he could pull away to his left, "in order to come on them from the east". Third, he could attempt a pincer movement with his battleship as one arm from the east, and Parona's cruisers as the other from the west.

The third choice might seem to be the most likely move; but to get into the right disposition, even with his superior speed, would take time, and would leave him with the possibility of a scattered force at the onset of darkness. He would risk neither a night action, as this was contrary to Italian policy, nor the hazards of destroyer attacks against a dispersed force. Perhaps for much the same reason he disliked the idea of a move to the east. The more direct manoeuvre was to intercept the convoy, which was now proceeding southwards, with his whole force from the west. There seemed little to stop him, except four light cruisers and a few destroyers, all of which could be destroyed by his 15in and 8in guns that easily outranged all the British guns.

"Thus began" writes Bragadin, "the second phase of the battle, lasting over two hours. Without exception the British ships continued to lay down smoke screens uninterruptedly until 19.30; that is until complete darkness had set in. As a result, an enormous mass of smoke arose between the enemy and the Italian ships. In it only fugitive glimpses were obtained of some of the British units. On their part, the British ships, immersed in that vast mass of smoke, manoeuvred more or less aimlessly and without any clear idea of the forces confronting them. Even their own reports occasionally speak of a 'mix-up'."

'Mix-up' there certainly was, owing to the difficulty of identifying even ships of the same division close up in the gathering murk. There was, however, no mix-up in the intentions of the British Admiral and those of his divisional leaders.

The direction of the wind was of great importance for it gave Vian's forces the weather gauge, the strong south-easterly vigorously blowing the thick smoke towards the enemy. A large area was soon covered with smoke which the Italians were unwilling to enter. Vian refers to "the enormous area of smoke", which lay well in the existing weather conditions. "The enemy" he wrote, "tried to make touch with the convoy by passing round the western edge of the smoke, to leeward, and was therefore effectually held away from the convoy, as he would not approach the smoke, which was drifting towards him".

Vian also noted that Iachino's most effective course of action would have been to pass to windward of the smoke, that is to the eastward of Vian's forces, instead of attempting what to them seemed the shortest route to the convoy. Because of only fleeting glimpses of the enemy through the smoke, there were occasions when Vian, and Grantham his flag captain, were unable to account for all the Italian ships to leeward: this led (three times during the action) to an eastward excursion for some minutes, by Vian, to ensure that no enemy ship was slipping round to attack the convoy from the windward side. Such an eastward excursion left grave risks on the battle-field, since Vian's division (*Cleopatra* and *Euryalus*), was closely followed and supported by McCall's division (*Dido* and *Penelope*) and Graham's division (*Zulu* and *Hasty*). This left the western flank open to any of the Italian ships that might decide to slip round to leeward: open, that is, except for the timely intervention of Micklethwait with his 5th division (*Sikh, Lively, Hero,* and *Havock*). The moves can be followed more clearly on Map 5. It can also be seen that Poland's 1st division (*Jervis, Kipling, Kelvin, Kingston,* and *Legion*) remained for some time with the convoy, as previously ordered, though at some distance astern of the merchant ships, in order

Right: Angelo Iachino later Admiral and C-in-C Italian fleet.

Below: Zara class: 8 inch Italian cruiser *Gorizia* (flag of Admiral Parona) Sunk at La Spezia 26.6.44 [*Gift of Italian Navy*

Top left: Trento class 8 inch Italian cruiser *Trento;* torpedoed by HM Submarine *Umbra* 15.6.42 [*Gift of Italian Navy*

Middle left: Soldati class Italian destroyers at Sirte: there were six like this one, the *Alfino, Ascari, Aviere, Bersagliere, Fuciliere, Lanciere.* The *Lanciere* foundered in storm 23.3.42 [*Gift of Italian Navy*

Bottom left: Oriani class Italian destroyer at Sirte: *Oriani* [*IWM*

Top right: HMS *Carlisle* (Neame): built 1918, converted to anti-aircraft cruiser World War II [*IWM*

Above right: Hunt class escort vessel: HMS *Avon Vale* (Withers) which with *Carlisle* comprised 6th division for smoke laying protection of convoy [*IWM*

Left: Penelope attempts to tow *Breconshire* into harbour when the supply ship is disabled by bombing off Malta 23.3.42 [*IWM*

Below: Breconshire successfully brings relief to Malta Jan '42 in an operation two months before Sirte [*IWM*

Above right: The Norwegian *Talabot* having safely arrived in the Grand Harbour, Malta, is hit 26.3.42 and has to be scuttled because of her cargo of ammunition [*IWM*

Below right: The *Pampas* sinking and burning fiercely in the Grand Harbour, Malta, after being hit 26.3.42 [*IWM*

Top: J class: HMS *Jervis* (Poland); 14th DF leader and 1st division leader 22.3.42. Led torpedo attack against *Littorio* [*IWM*

Above: K class: HMS *Kipling* (St Clair-Ford); 14th DF and 1st division 22.3.42 . This picture shows her being cheered on entering Alexandria in the previous year after a particularly gallant withdrawal of troops from Crete May 41. [*IWM*

Top right: K class: HMS *Kelvin* (Allison); 14th DF and 1st division 22.3.42 [*IWM*

Middle right: K class: HMS *Kingston* (Somerville); 14th DF and 1st division 22.3.42. Hit by *Littorio*. Bombed in dock at Malta 11.4.42 [*IWM*

Bottom right: L class: HMS *Legion* (Jessel) attached to 1st division 22.3.42. Bombed in dock at Malta 26.3.42 [*IWM*

BATTLE OF SIRTE

23 March 1942.

To: Admiral Sir Andrew Cunningham, K.C.B., D.S.O.
Commander-in-Chief, Mediterranean Fleet.

'I shall be glad if you will convey to Admiral Vian, and all who sailed with him, the admiration which I feel at this resolute and brilliant action by which the Malta convoy was saved.

That one of the most powerful modern battleships afloat, attended by two heavy and four light cruisers and a flotilla of destroyers should have been routed and put to flight with severe torpedo and gunfire injury, in broad daylight, by a force of five British light cruisers and destroyers, constitutes a naval episode of the highest distinction and entitles all ranks and ratings concerned and above all their commander to the compliments of the British nation.'

Winston S. Churchill

Ships taking part:

Rear Admiral P. L. Vian, D.S.O., Commanding the 15th Cruiser Squadron flying his Flag in H.M.S. "Cleopatra," Captain G. Grantham, D.S.O., R.N.
H.M.S. "Euryalus," Captain E. W. Bush, D.S.O., D.S.C., R.N.
H.M.S. "Dido," Captain H. W. M. McCall, R.N.
H.M.S. "Carlisle," Captain D. M. L. Neame, D.S.O., R.N.
H.M.S. "Penelope," Captain A. D. Nichols, D.S.O., R.N.
14th Destroyer Flotilla, Captain (D) A. L. Poland, D.S.O., D.S.C., R.N.
22nd Destroyer Flotilla, Captain (D) St. J. A. Micklethwait, D.S.O., R.N.

not to be too far removed from the surface action which was now imminent.

The *Cleopatra* and *Euryalus,* having led out in line ahead on an intercepting course to the northward at 16.40, began immediately to lay smoke, closely followed by *Dido* and *Penelope* in line ahead on their starboard quarter.

At 16.43 *Cleopatra* and *Euryalus* opened fire individually on the westernmost 8in cruiser, at a range of 20,000 yards, ie 10 sea miles. This was approaching the limit of their range (see Appendix E).

The Italian cruisers immediately returned the fire, finding the British ships easily within range of the Italian guns. The 6in *Bande Nere* then hit the *Cleopatra* with her second salvo. This killed one officer and 14 ratings on the starboard side of the Air Defence Position, and seriously wounded an officer and four ratings. The ship's radio and radar were also put out of action. In addition to the casualties from this direct hit, near misses killed one rating and caused structural damage.

The Italian battleship *Littorio,* outside the range of the British ships, now opened fire. A splinter from her 15in shells hit the *Euryalus.* Her captain, Bush, writes (in *Bless Our Ship*), "We were in for something now all right! I knew that Admiral Vian would never leave the convoy to its fate, so if needs be we would be fighting to the end . . . *Cleopatra* had been hit on the bridge by a 6in shell, but steamed on unaffected . . .

"Then the *Littorio* spotted *Euryalus* through a gap in the smoke screen. I saw flashes from her 15in guns rippling down her side as she fired a salvo at us. An age seemed to pass before her shells arrived with a deafening crash, as they plunged into the water all round us, engulfing the ship in columns of water masthead high. We'd been straddled! . . . Fragments of shell screamed through the air to bury themselves in our ship's sides."

But Bush's response was swift. With a 'Starboard 20', he was able to alter the range before the next salvo arrived. But the fire from the Italian heavy ships was not the only peril, for the cruisers were being attacked from the air at the same time.

In the *Cleopatra,* the flag captain, Grantham, was similarly faced with ship handling problems, and also with the additional role of attendance on the Admiral. He writes:

"An almost continuous smoke screen was used to shield the convoy and its Hunt class escort, and for much of the time *Cleopatra,* from before the foremost funnel, was showing ahead of the black cloud, except when doubling back and before popping out again to see what the Italian ships were doing.

"We got a lot of the gunfire and being close straddled by 15in shells was quite a noisy experience — they made a tremendous bang when they hit the water.

"At the same time we were being bombed and we could see the convoy being attacked by many waves of bombers. We used our three forward turrets for firing at the enemy ships, and the two after turrets against aircraft.

"We in *Cleopatra* were only hit once. It was a 6in shell, which I saw coming, apparently straight at me, though it sheered off at the last moment and hit the starboard fore corner of the bridge, where Philip Vian normally stood or sat on his stool chair. I was in my usual position, port fore corner; he was luckily having a quick look at our position in the charthouse. That shell killed an officer and 14 men, and brought down all our radio aerials. But it did not harm the main armament director, and we were able to continue firing normally."

Bush, in *Euryalus,* just astern of the *Cleopatra,* writes:

"Again came the flash of guns and the seemingly endless time of flight while we knew that this might be the end of us. But luck was on our side, for the salvo passed harmlessly over and burst in the water beyond.

"Then *Cleopatra* led round to port. *Littorio* disappeared behind the smoke screen. We could breathe freely again."

It was 16.48 when Vian led round westward into the smoke screen, followed by *Euryalus,* and then ceased fire; only eight minutes after the Italian ships had been sighted. Meanwhile, Captain McCall's division, the *Dido* and *Penelope,* had also come into action. They found it difficult to observe their fall of shot owing to the smoke and spray; and neither they, nor the *Cleopatra* and *Euryalus,* could claim a hit on the enemy at this stage of the battle. When Vian turned away, *Dido* and *Penelope* followed him into the smoke, and momentarily lost sight of him.

"That we survived" writes McCall, "was mainly due to the weather, lowering cloud with a strong south-easterly wind which increased to gale force and which provided ideal conditions for smoke-laying.

"Outside the smoke screen, visibility was good. Time and time again we dashed out to sight the enemy and fire a few salvoes. When enemy shells got too close, we retreated under the blanket, altering course as soon as we were unobserved, to mislead the enemy.

"Thanks to these tactics, and any amount of good fortune, neither my ship nor *Penelope* was hit."

In his report Captain McCall said:

"The smoke was at that time extremely dense; 15in guns could be heard firing at no great distance, occasional large splashes were seen, and the positions of destroyers were obscure; so that a very exciting period ensued ... until we emerged from the smoke, steering an easterly course, at 17.03, when the enemy cruisers were sighted, (probably in loose line abreast according to the official report), on a south-westerly course with the battleship three miles to the east of them on a westerly course."

Map 5 shows approximately the tracks between the movement of sighting at 16.40 and 17.40, and indicates the first of Vian's excursions to the eastward which he undertook at 17.05 to ensure that none of the Italian ships should get to windward of the smoke and thus find a relatively easy path to the convoy.

"Following an engagement in a clear area with the cruisers", writes Vian in *Action This Day,* "Captain Grantham pointed out that not all the enemy ships which had at various times been seen were then visible. I therefore turned eastward, taking a division with me, thinking the missing ships must have doubled round behind the convoy."

In the first instance between 17.00 and 17.15 his detour was of little significance, though as he had with him in addition to the *Cleopatra* division, both the *Dido* division and the *Zulu* division (the destroyers *Zulu* and *Hasty* under Commander Graham), the situation was such that the *Sikh* division under Captain Micklethwait was the only force left to hold the field. The *Jervis* division under Captain Poland was still well to the south-east of the scene supporting the Hunts in their role of repelling air attacks on the convoy.

In the next instance, however, when Vian made his second detour south-eastward, beginning at about 17.20, the situation could have become very serious. The Italian ships gained bearing on the convoy, and the chance of a gap in the smoke screen arose. It was then left to the British destroyers to come to the rescue in the nick of time. Their movements will be covered in the next chapter.

CHAPTER NINE

The Convoy in Peril

Captain Micklethwait with the *Sikh* division had, since the sighting at 16.40 been steaming westward in the smoke on a course slightly converging on that of the Italian ships and in a position broad on their bow (see Map 5). By 16.49 he was some distance to the westward of Vian's cruisers who had just had their first encounter. At this moment Micklethwait sighted two of the Italian cruisers and the battleship bearing north-east, distant six miles, so he hurried westward with his division to gain a more favourable position for launching torpedoes. But after 10 minutes, the Italian group, this time cruisers only, appeared to be still on the same bearing distant five miles. Micklethwait in the *Sikh* then altered course to the north-west, and engaged the group with his four destroyers for six minutes, making use of smoke as necessary, until the battleship again came in sight. At 17.05 he turned away to the south "to avoid punishment".

Micklethwait's division did not escape punishment, however, for at 17.20 the *Havock* received a near miss from a 15in shell fired by the *Littorio* which damaged a boiler, and restricted her speed to 16 knots. Two officers and five ratings were killed, one officer and eight ratings were wounded, and No 3 boiler room was flooded. *Havock* was thereupon sent south to join the convoy.

By this time, 17.20, Vian was beginning his second detour to the south-east, and it was to be 15 long minutes before he stopped his excursion eastward and turned to a westerly course at 17.35. By then he was six miles south-eastward of Micklethwait's three destroyers, and 14 miles from the Italian ships. Vian realised that this was a grim predicament, for although the Italian ships were outside the range of his four cruisers, the convoy was well within the range of the Italian battleship. And if the smoke should blow clear nothing could save the merchantmen.

After the *Havock* had been detached, Micklethwait turned northwards for a few minutes with a view to attacking with torpedoes, but as the range was too great and other factors unfavourable, he shaped a course to the southward, intent on laying smoke to prevent the Italian ships from sighting the convoy.

Micklethwait's division now opened fire on the battleship; *Sikh* with her eight 4.7in, *Hero* with her five 4.7in, and *Lively* with her eight 4in guns. Micklethwait commended the manner

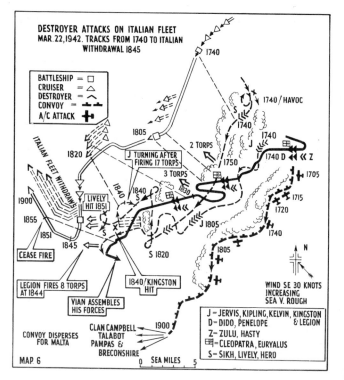

DESTROYER ATTACKS ON ITALIAN FLEET
MAR. 22, 1942. TRACKS FROM 1740 TO ITALIAN
WITHDRAWAL 1845

BATTLESHIP = □
CRUISER = △
DESTROYER = ⌃
CONVOY =
A/C ATTACK = ✚

ITALIAN FLEET WITHDRAWS

1740
1740 / HAVOC
1805
2 TORPS
1820
J TURNING AFTER FIRING 17 TORPS
1840
3 TORPS
1750
1740
1740 D
Z
1705
1715
1720
1900
1830
1840
1840
LIVELY HIT 1851
1855
1851
1845
CEASE FIRE
J 1805
S 1820
1840 / KINGSTON HIT
1740
1805

WIND SE 30 KNOTS
INCREASING
SEA V. ROUGH

N

LEGION FIRES 8 TORPS
AT 1844

VIAN ASSEMBLES
HIS FORCES

CLAN CAMPBELL
TALABOT
PAMPAS &
BRECONSHIRE

1900

CONVOY DISPERSES
FOR MALTA

MAP 6

0   SEA MILES   5

J = JERVIS, KIPLING, KELVIN, KINGSTON
D = DIDO, PENELOPE   & LEGION
Z = ZULU, HASTY
⊞ = CLEOPATRA, EURYALUS
S = SIKH, LIVELY, HERO

in which the *Hero* and *Lively* followed astern of the *Sikh* through salvoes of both large and small shell fire. The range was too great for them to observe their own fall of shot; and in any case *Sikh's* smoke screen, between them and the enemy, prevented them from seeing much of the action. Great seas sweeping over the forecastles added to the difficulties, and there was violent rolling and pitching. Nevertheless the Italians say that the *Littorio* was frequently straddled, though not hit, and momentarily turned away to open the range. As a measure of the defiance of Micklethwait's small force of destroyers, it should be remembered that the *Littorio* had in addition to her main armament of nine 15in guns, a secondary armament of twelve 6in (whose maximum range was more than 12 miles), and four 4.7in guns. (For ranges of guns of the British ships, see Appendix E; Italian ships, Appendix C).

Littorio was returning the fire, and at 17.48 straddled the *Sikh*. The battleship appeared to be gaining rapidly on the convoy which from 17.40 was steering westward. Micklethwait's response was to fire two of his four starboard torpedoes, though the range was too great for much promise of a hit. His hope was to make the *Littorio* turn away, and he was resolved anyway not to be sunk with all torpedoes on board.

By 18.05 the Italians were clearly gaining on the convoy, and it required only a gap in the smoke screen for the merchantmen to be revealed on a converging course at an easy distance of only 11 miles, easy that is, for both the secondary and main armaments of the *Littorio*.

Micklethwait continued his "somewhat unequal contest" with the enemy, while doing his utmost to extend the smoke screen westward. In the absence of Vian he made a signal to the convoy to alter course to the southward. This at any rate would delay the fate of the convoy whose utter destruction now appeared to be imminent.

Meanwhile at 17.35, Vian, realising the peril which now faced the convoy, and satisfied that none of the Italian vessels would for the moment endanger his eastern flank, had turned westward to speed to the assistance of Micklethwait's destroyer division. Vian's own cruiser division (*Cleopatra* and *Euryalus*) was closely followed by McCall's cruiser division

(*Dido* and *Penelope*), and Graham's destroyer division (*Zulu* and *Hasty*).

At 17.42 *Cleopatra* caught a glimpse of the battleship *Littorio* bearing north-west, distant 12 miles, and fired salvoes at extreme range before being swallowed up in smoke. This smoke covered all Vian's ships and lasted for 20 minutes, despite his attempts to cut a way into the clear so as to get a sight of the enemy. Frustrated by his own smoke in attempts to shoot at the enemy, Vian determined to make use of the smoke cover for a combined torpedo attack in order to relieve pressure on Micklethwait. "Using a jury wireless mast which had now been erected" he recorded, "I ordered cruisers and destroyers to prepare to attack with their remaining torpedoes, if possible using smoke as cover."

That signal was made at 17.59. Three minutes later at 18.02, the *Cleopatra* cleared the smoke, sighted the battleship only 6½ miles away, and opened fire with all her turrets. The *Euryalus*, still in smoke astern of her, opened fire by radar direction. *Cleopatra* then turned to port, and at 18.06, fired her starboard torpedoes. Almost at once the battleship disappeared behind smoke, thus preventing observation of any possible hits, and frustrating any further firing.

Although hits were unlikely at this long range, the enemy had turned away at the threat of torpedoes.

By this time, 18.06, Poland's division of five destroyers was well on the way to support Micklethwait, and he was only eight miles from the *Littorio* on approximately parallel tracks to the south-west (see Map 6). It was shortly after this that Vian having steamed roughly west-south-westward for more than half an hour, once again became concerned about his eastern flank, and having seen the Italians turn away as a result of his torpedo attack, he decided that this was the time for another jog to the east. By 18.17 he could see that all was clear to the north-east, and resumed his westerly course in support of Micklethwait whose *Sikh* division turned northward at 18.20 to lay a fresh smoke screen.

Fresh smoke became essential, because the Italians, in spite of their turn away, were step by step approaching on a more southerly course which would give them more direct access to the convoy. Only Vian's cruisers and destroyers could stop them, and, but for the smoke, these could easily be outranged and kept off.

If the Italians could break through the smoke they would shortly be in a position to annihilate the British convoy.

CHAPTER TEN

Audacity Rewarded

It was at 18.20 that Captain Micklethwait, having ceased fire, made a complete turn to port and steamed northward to lay a new screen of smoke between the Italian ships and the convoy. With the *Hero* and *Lively* in company, *Sikh* continued on a northerly course till 18.35 and then turned south-west. (See Map 6).

By this time, the five destroyers of the *Jervis* division under Captain Poland, were in position to launch their combined torpedo attack.

It may be recalled that by 18.06 Poland's division was hastening to the support of Micklethwait. His first view of the battle was at 17.45 when he saw gun flashes to the north-west. Through the smoke being laid by Micklethwait's three destroyers he could see that that division was under heavy fire from 15in guns. A few minutes earlier he had caught a glimpse of the *Cleopatra* who flashed him by light, a signal "Feint at ..." before she disappeared into smoke. This he felt released him from the instructions to stand by the convoy, and permitted him to join battle against the Italian ships.

At 18.08 Poland received a signal (originated by Micklethwait at 17.58) that the Italians were only eight miles from the convoy. Actually this was an underestimate of three miles, for the distance was nearer 11 miles. Poland immediately altered course from south-west to north-west and then round to south and eventually west, frustrated not only by smoke in his search for the enemy ships but also by an attack by torpedo aircraft.

Suddenly at 18.34, while steaming north, Poland sighted the *Littorio* bearing west-north-west, six miles away, and decided on an immediate attack with torpedoes. His division, steaming north in line ahead in the order *Jervis, Kipling,*

Kelvin, Kingston, and *Legion,* now turned together to west, bringing his ships in line abreast. Speed was increased to 28 knots, and all the destroyers opened fire with their guns as they closed the *Littorio,* the first carrying out a concentration shoot on the battleship with their 4.7in guns. The *Legion* with her 4in, deferred opening fire until the range dropped to 4 miles. The destroyers were now closing at the rate of a mile every two minutes. The Italians were steaming south, in line ahead, with the battleship ahead of the three cruisers.

All the Italian ships returned the fire of Poland's destroyers, and this fire was reported by Captain Poland to be "very erratic". The erratic nature of the fire was probably due to the fact that by 18.30, Vian was hurrying westward again, after his third excursion to the east, and was now distant only 10 miles from the Italian ships. The *Cleopatra* sighted an enemy cruiser at 18.30 and exchanged salvoes until the smoke of Micklethwait's 5th division obscured the view. Five minutes later at 18.35 all four of the Italian ships came into view steaming south, and an exchange of fire between them and Vian's 2nd division then continued for 20 minutes during the first part of which Poland was carrying out his torpedo attack. (See Map 6).

"Our destroyers" writes Nicholl of the *Penelope,* "carried out their attacks on the *Littorio* with the greatest determination, plunging through heavy seas. They ran clear of our protecting smoke when about seven miles from the enemy but held on until the range was under three miles before turning to fire their torpedoes."

Here is an extract of the story told in Poland's words. "The moment seemed propitious for a torpedo attack on the enemy through the smoke made by Micklethwait's *Sikh* division. Accordingly I led round so as to pass astern of him and through his smoke while it was not too thick. When we emerged from the smoke we could see only one enemy ship which, instead of being four miles north-north-west of us, (as signalled by Micklethwait), was well over six miles away and bearing about west-north-west. The ship in sight also looked rather larger than the Italian 6in cruiser we had expected to see. However, the flotilla was ordered to take up formation for a torpedo attack and speed was increased to the maximum. Unfortunately some Italian torpedo bombers chose this moment to make an attack on us and we had to turn to comb the tracks of their torpedoes. This delayed us and had an adverse effect on our position relative to the enemy!

"It was very soon after passing through the smoke that a second enemy ship appeared out of the haze, also looking remarkably large, and a third, and a fourth. They also appeared to be an uncomfortably long way off and I remember inquiring more than once what the range of the nearest one was. The range seemed to close astonishingly slowly; the intervals between the ships seemed to be about three-quarters of a mile. They opened fire on us. My division opened fire with all the guns that would bear. Our cruisers were following us to support the attack, and firing as well.

"We went in in broad port quarter line, in the order *Jervis*, *Kipling*, *Kelvin*, *Kingston*, *Legion*. The range seemed to take an unconscionably long time to shorten, the fact being that we had not started, as we expected to do, from fine on the bow of the enemy, but from very broad on his bow; and so our rate of approach was much reduced. When the range of the nearest enemy from the *Jervis* was about 3½ miles it was grand to see the second ship in the enemy line lose her nerve. She turned and steered straight away from us, making volumes of black smoke.

"Eventually the range was down from the six miles to two and three miles for which we had been waiting (one of the longest three miles I have ever steamed). We turned, and some 25 torpedoes started off towards the enemy line."

This turn took place at 18.41, the first four destroyers turning to starboard. *Legion*, however, the last in the line, turned to port. Because her commanding officer wished to gain bearing, he had made the approach a little south of the westerly course steered by the first four, and owing to shell splashes he did not see the divisional leader's signal to turn to starboard. He was, however, able to fire all eight of his torpedoes.

The *Jervis* and *Kipling* each fired five torpedoes; and *Kelvin* fired four, though two of these were fired in error at 18.35, at the beginning of the run in, when the range was six miles, due to mistaking the signal to turn for the run in, for a signal to fire.

The *Kingston* was hit by a 15in shell as she was about to turn to fire, but nevertheless managed to get off three torpedoes. The shell passed through the ship and exploded outside. The upper deck suffered severely; pom-pom, oerlikon, and searchlight supports were damaged; a fire broke out in the boiler room but was extinguished. One officer and 12 ratings were killed; 21 ratings were wounded.

It is of interest to see the attack through other eyes. The captain of the *Kipling,* Commander Aubrey St Clair-Ford wrote:

"Captain Poland led his 1st division through the smoke screen, all of us wondering what we were going to see when we got to the other side.

"As we emerged, we sighted the *Littorio* class battleship, two 8in cruisers, and one 6in cruiser, in line ahead six miles away. I must admit I had hoped they would be closer and that we should be able to deliver our attack straight away and retire into the cover of the smoke screen, for it looked a sticky proposition closing the range whilst under fire from the main armament of these four large ships.

"However we crashed on at full speed and luckily the wind and sea were behind us. It went exactly like a peace time practice except for the disconcerting gun flashes from the enemy and the subsequent whine and splash of the falling shells.

"The 1st division closed to three miles range before turning to fire their torpedoes, but owing to the foul weather a lot of the electrical system was put out of action and again the years of peace-time practice bore their fruit, for although the torpedo firing circuits did not work, *Kipling's* five torpedoes were fired by hand at the tubes, at the correct time and target.

"After the torpedoes had been fired, the 1st division retired under cover of their own smoke, whilst Captain Micklethwait in the *Sikh* led his 5th division in for the attack."

The commanding officer of the *Kipling* makes it all sound so practised and dependable, and calls attention appropriately enough to Rudyard Kipling's "The Nurses", which he had had engraved on brassplates on commissioning HMS *Kipling*.

> These have so utterly mastered their work
> that work without thinking,
> Holding three-fifths of their brain in reserve
> for whatever betide.
> So, when catastrophe threatens of colic,
> collision or sinking,
> They shunt the full gear into train, and take
> that small thing in their stride.

Another who shared the thrill of the 1st division's torpedo attack on the Italian fleet was the engineer officer of the *Kelvin*, Lt-Cdr I. G. Aylen, who writes:

"It was very rough as we were battling along at nearly 30 knots, tired, hungry, and very wet, the torpedo-tubes' crew perched over their five lethal charges, waiting, as always, for the order to fire that never seemed to come. The guns' crews were constantly firing in anger. The asdic and radar teams were horribly active. The depth charge operators released their devastation often enough. But torpedoes, never!

"Each ship down the line burst forth its black smoke through which the 1st division was to attack. But attack what? There had been a brief engagement earlier. Had they returned?

"We didn't have long to wait. We plunged into the smoke, lethal choking stuff that stung the eyes. Then suddenly we came into the open sea again, wave-torn and angry, a black cloud astern of us. To port, a sudden chilling sight: an Italian battleship, but six miles distant. Great waterspouts shot up ahead of us, and suddenly one larger than the rest towered above us. Transfixed I watched it rise and rise, then suddenly as we tore through the water towards it, down it came, tons and tons.

"Then the tension dramatically eased with the order to 'Stand by the torpedo tubes'! A single torpedo leapt out, pursued much later by its four mates. And then the wait – it seemed like minutes – until a brilliant yellow and red flash rose from the battleship. Someone had scored a hit ... subsequent analysis showed conclusively that it was *only Kelvin's* first torpedo that could possibly have hit!"

There were one or two claims by individual destroyers who believed that they had scored a hit. But in fact not one of the

25 torpedoes that were fired found its target. Nevertheless, the *Littorio* immediately turned away at 18.41 as torpedoes were being fired. She was soon followed to the north west by the Italian cruisers. (See Map 6). The *Littorio* was seen at 18.41 to be on fire from a shell hit abaft her after turret. More hits were seen as she withdrew.

As Poland's 1st division retired to the east under smoke at 18.41, Micklethwait's 5th division prepared for an attack. "We were still doing 28 knots when we turned away", says Poland, "but as we had to turn head into the wind and sea we very quickly had to reduce to 20 knots. The few moments before we did so brought about four green seas over the forecastle and drowned us with spray on the bridge.

"The *Kingston*, hit in the engine room and boiler room, just managed to get torpedoes off before coming to a full stop. Her captain and crew did grand work and got her going again. I sent her off to join the convoy so as to get to Malta for repairs.

"Meanwhile the 5th division had turned to make a torpedo attack when we had finished, but found the enemy going 'hell for leather' north-west and out of torpedo range. He reported a hit as of a torpedo on the end ship, and we in the *Jervis* were firmly convinced that it was one of our torpedoes."

It will be recalled that Micklethwait, virtually alone with his *Sikh*, *Hero*, and *Lively*, had ceased fire at 18.19, before turning and proceeding northwards for a quarter of an hour, to lay a new smoke screen to prevent *Littorio* from sighting the convoy. And at 18.35 he made a complete turn to starboard and assumed a course to the south-west.

As soon as the Italian ships began at 18.41 to turn away to the north-west it was evident to Micklethwait that he could quickly put himself into an advantageous position for a torpedo attack. Unfortunately as he turned to fire at 18.55, thick smoke hid the target from both *Sikh* and *Hero*. *Lively*, however, was able to fire eight torpedoes. But the range was about four miles, and all torpedoes missed. *Lively* for her pains was hit at the moment she was about to fire, by the splinter of a 15in shell. There was some flooding, but she suffered no casualties.

Commander Fisher of the *Hero*, wrote:

"Another picture I recall is passing close to the *Kingston*;

71

stopped, and on fire somewhere aft. Somerville, [her Commanding Officer],was signalling rather pleadingly that he was disabled. I think we replied, as we disappeared again in the smoke, 'We'll come back when we've driven off the enemy' (or words to that effect).

"Then there was a moment when *Sikh* led us out of the smoke to see momentarily, large Italian ships. By the time *Hero* came to the turning point before diving back into the smoke, I thought I could see the enemy ships turning away, and did not waste my torpedoes on such a poor target.

"I was under the impression that there would be much more profitable use for them during the coming night".

But the 1st and 5th divisions had achieved the object by their torpedo attacks.

"At sundown" writes Cdr Bragadin, "when the darkness

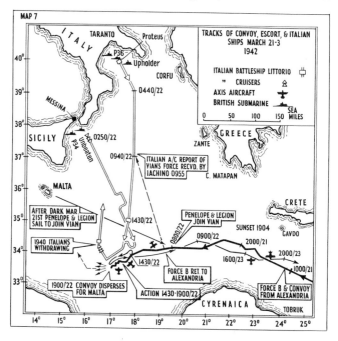

MAP 7

TRACKS OF CONVOY, ESCORT, & ITALIAN
SHIPS MARCH 21-3
1942

ITALIAN BATTLESHIP LITTORIO
"   CRUISERS
AXIS AIRCRAFT
BRITISH SUBMARINE

0   50   100   150   SEA MILES

TARANTO   Proteus
ITALY
P36
Upholder
CORFU
0440/22
MESSINA
0250/22
SICILY   Unbeaten
0940/22   ITALIAN A/C REPORT OF
VIANS FORCE RECVD. BY
IACHINO 0955
C. MATAPAN
GREECE
ZANTE
MALTA
CRETE
AFTER DARK MAR
21ST PENELOPE & LEGION
SAIL TO JOIN VIAN
1430/22
PENELOPE & LEGION
JOIN VIAN
SUNSET 1904   GAVDO
0900/22   2000/21
1940 ITALIANS
WITHDRAWING
1600/23   2000/23
1430/22   1000/21
FORCE B RET. TO
ALEXANDRIA   FORCE B & CONVOY
FROM ALEXANDRIA
1900/22 CONVOY DISPERSES
FOR MALTA   ACTION 1430-1900/22
CYRENAICA   TOBRUK

72

was rapidly deepening, Admiral Iachino realised that the action had to be considered ended."

Having turned away at 18.40, he had by 18.51 assumed a course for his fleet to the north-west. The last shots were fired at 18.56. As the sun set (at 19.04) on that Passion Sunday, March 22nd, 1942, Vian at last saw the enemy abandon their struggle and steer for home. This was the turning point of the battle.

Grantham writes, "I had forgotten to wind my watch the night before and the day seemed endless. When we were getting low in ammunition I looked at my watch, and said to the Admiral, 'I don't think we shall have enough rounds to last until dark'. It was heavily overcast at the time and he said it would be dark in under half an hour, as of course it was. The enemy withdrew at high speed at dusk."

The battle was over for the time being. As soon as the Italian ships had disappeared in the twilight Vian collected his ships and made for the convoy 10 miles to the southward.

CHAPTER ELEVEN

Each To His Destination

The British naval Commander-in-Chief had been watching the progress of the battle on the plot in his war room at Alexandria, knowing how fraught with danger every minute of the situation was until darkness descended. Lt-Col Moseley describes him pacing up and down. "Then the dramatic claim of a hit, and A.B.C's joy." "Finally" says Moseley, "Vian's night dispositions and intention to withdraw. Here A.B.C. intervened for the first time, saying 'The convoy will need the *Carlisle's* anti-aircraft protection entering Malta, we must instruct Vian to detach her'."

Cunningham refers to the indescribable relief when he heard that the Italians were withdrawing. In order to lighten Vian's responsibility he signalled him to the effect that doubtless he, Vian, had already considered dispersing the convoy in order that the ships could make their way individually to Malta as fast as they could steam.

It will be recalled that Vian had collected his force as soon as the Italian ships had withdrawn, and steered southward to close the convoy. At 19.40, in the growing darkness and with the convoy not yet in sight, he decided that not only would he send the convoy on to Malta, but would himself shape course immediately for Alexandria with Force B. The Italian ships were retiring northward to home ports, and were unlikely to risk a night attack on the ships of the convoy. "The weather was strong south-easterly to east-south-easterly gale, with a rising sea and swell," said Vian in his dispatch. "Fuel in the K class and Hunt class destroyers were insufficient to allow an extra day to be spent in the central basin west of Benghazi, so it was necessary for us to get as far east as possible through Bomb Alley before daylight." See Appendix J.

Captain Hutchison of the *Breconshire* had, as commodore

of the convoy, complied with the operation orders on his own initiative at 19.00 and had dispersed the ships on diverging courses with the hope that at least some of the valuable cargo would reach Malta.

"My plan for dispersal," writes Hutchison, "was based on the speed of the ships; thus *Clan Campbell*, being the slowest, was to proceed direct to the end of the swept channel to Malta. *Talabot, Pampas, Breconshire* were to make legs to the southward, the amount of diversion depending upon the speed of the ships, and the idea was that at daylight on Monday, March 23rd the convoy would again be concentrated and in the swept channel, with *Carlisle* and the close escort to look after them." The principle of concentrating ships and their escorts during daylight, in order the more effectively to repel air attack, had become an accepted policy.

The plight of the four ships of the convoy during the four hours of the afternoon of Passion Sunday should be realised. Compared with the warships of their close escort, they were relatively defenceless and could only hope that their escort's gunfire and their own manoeuvring would be sufficient to keep them unharmed by the almost continuous air attacks. Nevertheless the *Breconshire* and *Pampas* each shot down an attacking bomber. None of the four ships of the convoy was hit or even damaged by near misses that afternoon. This is a remarkable testimony to the effectiveness of the firing by the ships of the close escort. Details of the Aircraft Background are given in Appendix H.

Captain D. R. J. Edkins, the Hampshire Regiment, was one of a party of twelve Army officers who took passage in SS *Talabot*. During the action he manned a Bren gun for most of the time. "Action Stations again about 2.15 with the arrival of Ju 88s" he writes, "The whole fleet opened up and the resultant barrage was most impressive, the din indescribable. The sky over the convoy was virtually obliterated by bursting 'shell-puffs'. The sea was really getting up but the sun was out most of the time and visibility was good. A stick of bombs came down apparently on the bows of the *Clan Campbell* but she emerged undamaged through great gouts of water. We got the second stick, about 'a number One wood' to starboard! Soon bombs were fairly whistling down, audible above the din of the barrage. The 88s were now diving much lower before releasing their bombs and for the first time we heard the chatter of the Bren guns, the coughs of the Bredas, and the wumps of the 4in. I saw one stick of bombs pitch almost certainly on the stern of the unfortunate Clan boat; but again she re-appeared from a curtain of water all in one piece. By 15.30 the weather had turned really foul and we were bouncing all over the place. A stick of four came crashing down to starboard, not more than 100 yards away. Not long afterwards I saw towering columns of water spouting out of the sea, grey at the base, becoming gradually white towards their pinacles. A tap on the shoulder and a huge mug of proffered tea and in splendid Norwegian tones, 'Fifteen inch shells. The Wop has sent out what you call a battle-waggon, no?'

"The 15in splashes were all over the place; the Italians didn't seem to have the range. The Navy now thickened up the smoke and we were dropping smoke-candles, the wind rolling the smoke towards the Italians. It was blowing like hell and, with the smoke and gun flashes, accentuated by the pervading gloom, Dante's Inferno had been reborn. It was incredibly thick smoke. How ships missed each other, dashing about in it, seemed a miracle to us. One sight I shall never forget; a cruiser belting along, parallel to the smoke, every detail etched out in silver by the sun before she disappeared into the murk. Only a flash, but unmistakably the *Penelope* with the seas going right over her quarter-deck. Then directly above us at about twelve thousand feet we saw six Ju 88s. They peeled off and we had our first dive-bombing attack. My Brens were loaded with part tracer and I got rid of four magazines at three of the enemy who each dropped a stick of four at us. I saw one stick, in my sights, actually spreading out before it was obscured by the funnel. I followed the 88 with tracer down the length of the ship. One of our Bredas got him – our first kill. Within minutes two more 88s came in but their aim was pretty wild. Finally a single 88 came down in a vertical dive; smoke was pouring out from one engine as he pulled out just in time to avoid the 'drink' with all of us pumping away at him broadside on. We chalked him up as a 'possible'. At about 17.00 the light began to fade and what looked like a possible torpedo attack came in out of the sun, Ju 88s and Savoias, very low. We didn't see any 'fish' but a Savoia came straight at us, only a couple of hundred feet above the sea. He began to wobble, banked round our bows and went straight into the sea. Shortly afterwards a 88 was shot down to end the party."

Captain Hutchison says that he regretted the turns to the southward which he had been ordered to carry out, "because we were getting over on to the coast of Africa instead of getting on towards Malta. On each occasion after about half an hour I turned back to the westward.

"Just about sunset I received a signal from Admiral Vian. Consequently I ordered the convoy to disperse in accordance with previous instructions. Two Hunts remained with me, and two Hunts with *Clan Campbell*. After dark I was joined by *Carlisle*."

The other ships to make for Malta after dark were the *Penelope* and *Legion* of Force K, still based in Malta, and the *Havock* and *Kingston* which were too badly damaged to return to Alexandria, especially in the face of the developing gale.

According to Hutchison, "the *Talabot* and the *Pampas* proceeded direct to Malta straight over the Italian minefield". Their good luck held, and though they failed to arrive at Malta before daylight, they both entered the Grand Harbour between 09.00 and 10.00 on Monday, March 23rd, the *Pampas* having been hit by two bombs neither of which exploded. Their escorts had by now used almost all their ammunition. In spite of the bombing at that moment, much of which was directed at the two new arrivals, the ships were given a tremendous welcome by the populace assembled in the various battlements which surround the Grand Harbour. The two ships steamed past the bastions to their deep water unloading berths at the southern end of the harbour, suffering gusts of gale force and unceasing bombing. Though their end was near, they had at least arrived.

The grand assault on Malta, as advocated by Admiral Raeder, was to be executed by Field-Marshal Kesselring. This had begun with an attempt at the preliminary neutralisation by bombing, only three days earlier on March 20th. It concentrated initially on the destruction of Malta's gun batteries and her airfields. Fliegerkorps II were now making an average of over 300 sorties a day despite bad weather. On this particular day, Monday, March 23rd, Malta's Spitfires and Hurricanes were unable to make more than 42 sorties in reply.

Enemy aircraft had appeared at first light, and despite the thick weather had made continuous attacks on the approaching supply ships whose escorts were so short of ammunition that they would only fire when danger was immediate. "Every aeroplane in Sicily seemed to be flying round the island" was the remark of the Air Officer Commanding, Malta.

The *Breconshire* was not so lucky as the *Pampas* and *Talabot,* having been hit and disabled at 09.20 only eight miles off Malta, after surviving a score of air attacks since daylight. She had been escorted by the *Carlisle* and three Hunts, the former of which now circled her to fight off bombers while preparing to take her in tow. The larger cruiser *Penelope* arrived on the scene and took over the difficult attempt at towing. The *Carlisle* was practically out of ammunition.

It was found, however, that because of the great draught of the damaged *Breconshire* and the heavy swell that was running, towing was impracticable. She was therefore anchored to prevent her being driven on shore, and provided with three Hunts for anti-aircraft protection. She was not far off Marsa Xlokk (pronounced Shlock and meaning Scirocco) a harbour at the south-east end of Malta.

Nicholl of the *Penelope* writes "the *Breconshire* was hit. Her engines were put out of action and she lost all electrical power. I ordered *Carlisle* to try to take her in tow but she was unable to do so. The *Penelope* then managed to pass a towing wire, but in the full gale this soon parted and *Breconshire* had to let go an anchor to avoid being blown ashore."

The slow *Clan Campbell* was more unfortunate than the others. Accompanied by the *Eridge,* she was 50 miles south-east of Malta at daylight when air attacks began. At 10.30 while still some 20 miles short of her destination, she was hit by a bomb; she sank soon afterwards. In spite of the heavy weather and the severe bombing, Lt-Cdr W. F. Gregory-Smith spent 2½ hours with his *Eridge* picking up 112 survivors; these constituted most of the crew of the bombed *Clan Campbell.*

So far on this day of approach to Malta, Monday, March 23rd, all the ships of war had escaped injury, but it was now the fate of the destroyer *Legion* of Force K to be damaged by a near miss when she was ordered to join the *Clan Campbell.* She had to be beached in Marsa Xlokk.

The convoy score then, on this wild Monday was two ships arrived in Grand Harbour; one ship anchored near Marsa Xlokk; one sunk.

Meanwhile the homeward bound Italian Fleet had not been free of misfortune, though they had escaped the attentions of a striking force of torpedo bombers which had been sent out to find them before dark on Sunday March 22nd, consisting of Beauforts of No 39 Squadron RAF from Egypt, and Albacores of No 828 Squadron FAA from Malta. And in spite of being heard by British submarines lying in wait for them off the Italian home ports, they could not be seen owing to the very poor visibility in heavy rain. The weather had worsened overnight to such an extent that two Italian destroyers, the *Scirocco* and the *Lanciere,* foundered on March 23rd, and the 6in cruiser *Bande Nere* suffered severe damage. The *Scirocco* was one of two destroyers that had been sent out from Taranto on March 22nd to join the *Littorio.*

Commander Bragadin refers to "battling against raging waves" and "the hurricane". "The God of the tempest" he writes, "had not only aided the British to escape the greatest of dangers during the encounter but had also sought to inflict painful punishment on the Italian Fleet ... Even the *Littorio* herself was making headway only with great difficulty and was suffering considerable damage."

The badly damaged *Bande Nere* managed to reach Messina on March 24th; but on passage to Spezia on April 1st for essential repairs, she was sunk by HM Submarine *Urge* commanded by Lt-Cdr Tomkinson, in a position south-east of Stromboli.

Admiral Iachino blamed the slender hull construction, inefficient water-tight bulkheads, and defective pumping arrangements as the cause of the extensive nature of the damage. Even the *Littorio* shipped tons of water which affected such important factors as the electric firing machinery of one of her 15in turrets.

Meanwhile, Vian returning with Force B to Alexandria, was steaming head on into the gale and was forced to reduce speed. He had started at 22 knots after dark on March 22nd, but soon had to reduce to 18, and then to 15 knots. His force consisted of the cruisers *Cleopatra, Dido,* and *Euryalus,* and the destroyers *Jervis, Kipling, Kelvin, Sikh, Lively, Hero, Zulu,* and *Hasty;* the damaged *Kingston* and *Havock,* together with the *Carlisle* and the six Hunts, having been sent to Malta with Force K.

By dawn March 23rd, the only destroyer still in company with Vian was the *Sikh,* the rest having fallen astern, and some of them having suffered damage in the heavy sea and swell. He had barely reached the longitude of Benghazi, and enemy shadowers were soon flying over. It was necessary to establish concentration of his force before the inevitable bombing began.

It is interesting to recount some of the personal accounts of those who experienced this rough night passage after the battle.

"Driving into the storm" writes Bush, the captain of the *Euryalus,* "speed had to be reduced to 18 knots at 21.30, and 15 knots at 03.30 the next morning. Even then the destroyers were unable to keep up, and Admiral Vian had to turn back to gather them in at daylight."

Aylen in the *Kelvin* wrote of the following sad episode: "After we had again made smoke and turned away [upon withdrawal from the torpedo attack] there occurred one of the inevitable tragedies of warfare which underline its futility. A young seaman was washed overboard. As always Allison's seamanship was superb. Immediately pulling out of line he approached to within yards of the poor fellow. It was much too rough to lower a boat, and try as he might it proved impossible to bring the ship's stern up into the wind. Every second meant increasing the distance to catch up with Vian, striving to hurry through Bomb Alley. After the third attempt he had to take the fateful decision which makes a captain's lot so unenviable; and on we passed at maximum speed."

Poland, withdrawing in the leader *Jervis* after the 1st division's torpedo attack, remembers "finding the *Kelvin* lying stopped. Thinking she had been damaged we asked if we could help. Her Commanding Officer replied that he was 'only picking up a man who had gone overboard'.

"That night was most unpleasant. We were belting into the sea and wind at the highest speed considered safe, which had to be reduced to 15 knots. The whole ship was completely flooded and the mess decks feet deep in water. However, it had to be done, as we were still very much in 'Tom Tiddler's Ground', and could expect heavy air attacks as long as we were there.

"Our force was split up into a number of small units all holding on to one another with their teeth during the night, which was particularly dark and unpleasant."

Aubrey St Clair-Ford driving the *Kipling* writes: "Vian drove the whole force as hard as he dared so as to get under cover of our own fighter protection by next morning. It was a ghastly night, for the ship was being shaken from stem to stern by the high seas and no passage was allowed on the upper deck. Everyone on board was wet to the skin and no supply of hot drinks or dry clothing could possibly be arranged. However, when dawn broke, the slightly scattered force reformed with the weather improving, and we were able to make better speed as the day wore on."

It will be recalled that R. L. Fisher, the captain of the *Hero*, had obtained permission to come out for a "breath of sea air", in the place of *Hero's* permanent captain, who had fallen sick. He writes of the passage back to Alexandria "in a strong gale from ahead":

"I remember" says Fisher, "Vian signalling 'Raise steam for full speed', and my having to reply that I couldn't do so, for *Hero*, unlike any of the other destroyers except *Havock,* had three boilers and she had been so grossly overworked and denied a proper refit in the past months that she was losing feed water much faster than she could distill more, and we had to pump one boiler empty to keep the other two going.

"It was abominably rough and we were continuously falling with tremendous crump into holes where the ocean was entirely missing. The shield of our foremost gun was, I remember, wrapped round the gun and training gear so tightly that nothing could be moved.

"*Hero* was, I think, the only ship present without radar. At

81

all events *we* didn't have any and it was pretty well impossible to keep station on a pitch dark night in such conditions. Having started the night as 'inside right' on the anti-submarine screen we found ourselves at dawn 'outside left' or thereabouts. The rest of the force must have been amused to see us on their radar screens wandering across their front."

In spite of shadowers, no air attacks developed until late in the afternoon at 16.10 when eight Ju 87s (the fast short-range Stukas) attacked and concentrated upon the *Lively* which had the day before been damaged by a 15in shell, and was now lagging astern. By "acting the part", as Vian put it, the *Lively* was able to escape further injury. With moderating weather, however, he pushed on eastward with increased speed after dark, and detached the *Lively* to Tobruk. Sporadic attacks by Ju 88s and torpedo bombers continued until dark but no ships were hit.

CHAPTER TWELVE

The Reckoning

We left the heavily-bombed and storm-tossed scene of Malta on that Monday, March 23rd, to follow the respective movements of Iachino and Vian. With the *Talabot* and *Pampas* both in the Grand Harbour at Malta, and the *Breconshire* anchored not far off the harbour of Marsa Xlokk at the south-east end of the island, it appeared that Operation MG 1 had been fairly successful. And so it would have been but for the poverty of Malta's scant and hard pressed fighter force and anti-aircraft defence, and her close proximity to Sicily.

"March 24th and 25th" writes Bragadin, "the Luftwaffe launched a series of raids over Malta, unprecedented in their violence".

This was an intensification of the grand assault which had begun on March 20th, and was now particularly aimed at the three surviving newly arrived supply ships; and on the airfields of Malta. The British fighters were greatly outnumbered, and made 175 sorties on the 24th, and over 300 on the 25th. During the hours of darkness, ground crews struggled to repair the damage inflicted by day.

In spite of continuing bad weather and repeated bombing attacks the *Breconshire* was towed to Marsa Xlokk on Wednesday March 25th, and the destroyer *Legion* was got to the same anchorage. Hurricanes and Spitfires fought valiantly to frustrate the daylight air assaults and at first were successful. The ships under attack were however in relatively exposed and accessible positions.

On Thursday March 26th, both *Talabot* and *Pampas* at the southern end of Grand Harbour were hit by bombs and sunk, the former having to be scuttled because of an uncontrollable fire which threatened her cargo of ammunition. The *Legion* was also sunk while on her way to the dockyard from Marsa

Xlokk. Nor was *Breconshire's* end far away, for on Friday, March 27th, she finally succumbed to further assault and sank in shallow water in Marsa Xlokk, having suffered continual attack for four days.

Some of *Breconshire's* precious oil fuel was saved but because of the depth of water in which the *Talabot* and *Pampas* settled in their unloading berths in Grand Harbour, only a fraction of their cargoes was saved. Of the 26,000 tons embarked in the ships at Alexandria, about 5,000 tons were unloaded at Malta. A further 2,500 tons were got ashore some time later.

Captain Grantham writes: "You will remember that the *Breconshire* reached Marsa Xlokk and was later sunk in shallow water. They got most of the stuff out of her. If the *Talabot* and *Pampas* had been deliberately beached at the top of Grand Harbour, they would have managed to unload practically everything they were carrying, and would have saved a big salvage operation after the war."

There were obviously many lessons to be learned and noted, for it was sad to realise that such a hazardous operation had successfully got the ships to the vicinity of Malta, only to lose the major portion of cargo, because of unsuitable berthing and the overpowering air assaults. More fighters were essential before another operation could be contemplated. Unloading had also been made more difficult because "stevedores had refused to work during 'red flag' periods of alert"; (Mediterranean and Middle East, Vol III, p 172). Men from the Services took over this task on March 31st, and worked day and night despite the air assault and the unusual nature of the work.

It is worth recording the views of the Captain of the *Breconshire,* whose gallant ship had given service to Malta far surpassing that of any other ship, and included six trips from Alexandria in the past year.

"In retrospect", writes Captain Hutchison, "it would seem to me that the Governor General Dobbie, made a mistake in asking for a convoy to be sent from Alexandria, when he knew that he could not give them air protection in the approaches to Malta, nor when in harbour. He should have been satisfied with *Breconshire* alone who could have been moored under the cliffs in Marsa Mxett [the Marsa Muscetto harbour immediately to the west of the steep stone bastions of Valetta], where she could have been protected by gunfire, and one or two of the fighters could have looked after her."

Hutchison was unlikely to forget the fact that the effective speed of the convoy had been sadly limited by the slow *Clan Campbell.* He considered that without such a handicap *Breconshire* could have made several more trips to Malta, "and provided that she could get into harbour by the crack of dawn she would have been reasonably safe, for the last 12 hours of the approach would have been in the dark".

Instead of abating after the sinking of the supply ships, the air assaults on Malta grew steadily worse, and it became necessary to clear the island of all surface ships except the local defence vessels. The *Carlisle* and the four Hunts, *Beaufort, Dulverton, Hurworth,* and *Eridge* sailed for Alexandria on Wednesday, March 25th, and the damaged *Avon Vale* sailed four days later for Gibraltar, with the cruiser *Aurora* that had been refitting in Malta dockyard. Of the ships present at Vian's action on Passion Sunday in the Gulf of Sirte, there remained two damaged destroyers *Havock* and *Kingston,* and the cruiser *Penelope* now the only ship left of the original Force K. The *Penelope* was badly damaged on Thursday, March 26th by near misses and then became the chief target in the heaviest air raids. Reference to the fate of these ships will be made in the next chapter.

In the meantime, we saw previously that, on the day following the Sirte action Admiral Vian had been compelled by the heavy seas to reduce speed in order that his destroyers could catch up without sustaining further damage. And in spite of the bad weather and considerable distance from bases, RAF Beaufighters had been able to afford protection from bombing attacks.

By dawn Tuesday, March 24th, Vian's force was able to increase to 26 knots, and after eluding an attack by two enemy torpedo-bombers, arrived at Alexandria soon after noon.

Admiral Cunningham's Staff Officer (Operations), Commander W. Woods, (later Admiral Sir Wilfrid Woods, GBE, KCB, DSO), writes:

"Admiral Vian arrived back at Alexandria to a tremendous reception by the ships in harbour. I was on the 'stern walk' with the C-in-C and chief of staff, and a moving moment it was. ABC was unnaturally silent at first, but then all his delight burst out, and he cheered with the rest of us".

ABC's initial restraint may be attributed to those days and long hours of suspense as the action story unfolded, ending with the return of the fleet he so dearly loved. There was also the realisation that this was to be the last operation that would take place under his direction, for it was proposed shortly to send him to Washington as the First Sea Lord's representative on the Combined Chiefs of Staff Committee there. He had made an imperishable reputation and was liked and admired by the Americans. He preferred action to discussion round a table, and disliked the prospect of leaving the Mediterranean Fleet when its fortune was at its lowest ebb. He was not then to know that he would return within seven months in command of all the Allied Naval Forces for the landings in North Africa.

"They had a wonderful reception" writes Cunningham referring to Vian's force, "being enthusiastically cheered by the crews of all the warships and merchant vessels in the harbour.

"I went on board the *Cleopatra* at once to congratulate the Rear-Admiral on his fine performance for which he was subsequently created a KBE ...

"Action and weather damage had taken a severe toll of the destroyers, and no more than two fleet destroyers remained immediately serviceable.

"I shall always consider the Battle of Sirte on March 22nd, 1942 as one of the most brilliant naval actions of the war, if not the most brilliant. Nor must the mistake be made of thinking the Italians were inefficient. Our destroyers were received by heavy and accurate gunfire, and it was only by the mercy of Providence that many of them were not sunk and still more severely damaged." (*A Sailor's Odyssey*, p 454).

Cunningham was not one to belittle the ability of his opposite number, Admiral Iachino, and shared his respect for the hazards involved in laying one's big ships open to destroyer attack.

Bush describes the arrival at Alexandria (*Bless Our Ship*, p 232):

"The 15th Cruiser Squadron arrived at 12.15 March 24th entering harbour in the order *Cleopatra*, *Euryalus*, and *Dido*, with the destroyers ahead, which was the usual practice. And then to our ears came the distant sounds of a siren wailing 'Air Raid Warning, Red'.

"But it was not that after all, and how we laughed. Alexandria had turned out to greet us as heroes with a grand chuck-up. Tugs and launches led us in, their crews, Egyptian and British, going quite mad, dancing round, cheering and throwing their caps in the air. Even the crews of the immobilised Vichy-French ships sat up and took notice."

Poland writes (*Men of Action* p 158):

"It was unfortunate that I should have chosen the moment when the C-in-C came on board the *Jervis* on our arrival, to have my first bath since leaving harbour on March 20th, and to have to greet him in a dressing gown." There is a picture, however, which shows Poland fully dressed, with ABC, presumably upon the latter's departure from *Jervis* after congratulating the flotilla.

St Clair-Ford says "It might have been Peace Day by the noise of every siren and whistle in the harbour being sounded, whilst all ships 'cleared lower deck' and cheered Admiral Vian and his battered little Squadron . . battered not so much from the results of enemy action but from the effects of the very heavy weather encountered during the battle and on the ensuing night, for all destroyers had sustained damage to their gun shields and leaks in the hull, and upper deck gear and superstructures were bent and distorted in places. As a result, all ships had to have a few days in harbour for their damage to be made good."

Shortly before arriving at Alexandria, Vian made the following signal:

General from C S 15

By your endeavours and those of our forces at Malta, the Italian Fleet failed to make contact with convoy, nor did the Axis air forces damage any ships until off Malta, notwithstanding the great scale of attack. No ship in our fleet has suffered from air attack which is a tribute to its gunnery and dexterity.

Above all Malta has received stores vital to the island's defence.

But this signal was of course originated before the sinkings of the supply ships at Malta on March 26th and 27th.

The relative strengths of the rival fleets on April 1st, 1942, were:

Italian   4 serviceable battleships
Fleet;   9 cruisers
        55 destroyers and torpedo boats
        50 submarines

British Mediterranean
Fleet;   4 cruisers
       15 destroyers
       25 submarines

The greatest difference between the two had been that the Italian fleet, in accordance with the policy of keeping a 'fleet in being', seldom went to sea, except along confined routes and for specific purposes such as covering Axis convoys to Tripoli and Benghazi, or for an assault on British ships in central waters, whereas the British fleet was more often at sea than in harbour. Nevertheless, without any capital ships, Cunningham's mastery was now very much in jeopardy. Despite this, British morale was high, and it can be attributed unquestionably to the magnificent leadership displayed by Cunningham during the previous three years, and in the availability of such first class commanders as Vian.

But let Captain Bush conclude this chapter to indicate the spirit that still prevailed:

"That night Admiral Vian dined his three cruiser captains ashore, giving us the best meal the town could produce. I struggled back on board shortly before midnight to find our ship's company still working with a determination characteristic of them. Even the idlers, to use an old naval expression, the doctor, paymaster, padre, stewards, and store-keepers, had their coats off and were bearing a hand to hoist on board 5.25in shells, boxes of pom-pom ammunition, heavy cases of stores, and all the reinforcements the ship needed. At 03.00 I was woken up by the sound of cheering, meaning the job was done, and *Euryalus* ready for sea."

CHAPTER THIRTEEN

Malta's Fate In The Balance

It was ironical that most of the vital supplies carried on convoy MW 10 should have reached hard-pressed Malta, only to be lost after arrival because of the lack of a fighter defence that could match the tremendous onslaught made by Fliegerkorps II and the Italian Air Force.

Paradoxically, in spite of what was believed at the time, there had been very few hits from guns during the battle in the Gulf of Sirte, and no torpedo hits. The ship losses all took place after the battle.

Despite Vian's great success in getting the convoy past the Italian fleet, credit must be given to Admiral Iachino for his tactical skill in barring the convoy's route to Malta. The Second Battle of Sirte was to become a classic example of a successful action by a materially inferior fleet which, by skill and great boldness, achieved its object of preventing the enemy from sighting the convoy, though at times well within range. Iachino chose the direct route to the convoy, and though driven off by torpedo attacks, and at times by the threat of a torpedo attack, was able to force the convoy to make repeated alterations to the south, thus effectively delaying the convoy's likely time of arrival until broad daylight the following morning, and thereby being largely instrumental in its ultimate destruction, owing to accumulating damage sustained by it before arrival.

It was now evident that further convoys would have no chance of getting into Malta until fighter defence was replenished. There was heavy toll daily of the Spitfires which had arrived in Malta during March, and as most of these had been destroyed by the middle of April, enemy air raids had to be met by Malta's anti-aircraft guns. It was still Kesselring's belief that Malta must succumb to repeated bombing, and although there were times during the island's brave struggle when it was suggested that Malta would have to be captured in an Axis seaborne and airborne attack, the memories of the Luftwaffe's considerable losses in the assault on Crete in May 1941 were sufficient to cause such plans to be set aside for the moment.

Although it became no longer practicable to retain surface ships at Malta, special cargoes were run in by British submarines *Parthian, Regent, Rorqual, Porpoise,* and *Cachalot,* and also the fast minelayer *Welshman.* The *Havock* was able to sail from Malta after dark on April 5th, bound for Gibraltar, but was unfortunate in running aground at high speed on the Tunisian coast the next morning when avoiding a minefield south of Cape Bon. Bragadin *(Italian Navy in World War II,* p 167) claims that she was torpedoed by the Italian submarine *Aradam.* The *Kingston,* the other destroyer damaged at Sirte, was still too defective to sail, and was bombed and destroyed in dock at Malta on April 11th. Her distinguished captain, Commander Philip Somerville, was killed at the same time.

The loss of these two ships was sadly felt. Both had performed gallant service at Crete, and in the case of *Havock* special service also at the Battle of Matapan.

The *Penelope's* survival was due to the co-operation of all and sundry in spite of the heaviest raids which followed her being hit on March 26th. She was docked at once, and it then became a race to complete repairs before the next bomb hit her. Ships staff, dockyard workmen, and volunteer welders from the Royal Engineers all joined in the effort to get *Penelope* seaworthy. And meanwhile her eight 4in anti-aircraft guns did yeoman service. The following is a diary of main events:

April 4th dock caisson and dock pump damaged, and *Penelope* is again hit.
April 5th dock masonry littered the decks and obstructed the supply of ammunition to the guns.
April 6th 4in guns nearly worn out, and the gunnery officer killed in a premature explosion.
April 8th final spurt to enable *Penelope* to sail after dark; ammunition running out as air attacks increase.

April 9th *Penelope* passes Cape Bon at dawn doing 27 knots and suffers frequent air attacks by high and low level bombers as well as torpedo bombers.

April 10th *Penelope* reaches Gibraltar, her captain, A. D. Nicholl, wounded, and her hull riddled with holes from bomb splinters.

Bragadin says the *Penelope* was blessed by good fortune. She certainly was; for attempts to destroy her on passage were made by 11 Italian torpedo planes, 6 bombers and 14 fighter-bombers, as well as by 12 German bombers. Fortune favours the brave. Such defiance as was shown in the face of so much disaster evinces admiration. It also produced confidence that the tide must soon turn, as turn it did.

The spirit of the British nation at this time is exemplified by a signal made by the Prime Minister, Mr Winston Churchill, to the Commander-in-Chief, Mediterranean Fleet, after the battle, and also in the granting of a battle honour to all those British ships which were present at the Second Battle of Sirte. The exact constitution of the enemy forces and the damage inflicted were not known at the time: and personal honours and awards were to be made later. See Appendix L.

The Prime Minister's message reads:

To: Admiral Sir Andrew Cunningham, KCB, DSO, Commander-in-Chief Mediterranean Fleet, March 23rd, 1942.

I shall be glad if you will convey to Admiral Vian, and all who sailed with him, the admiration which I feel at this resolute and brilliant action by which the Malta convoy was saved.

That one of the most powerful modern battleships afloat, attended by two heavy and four light cruisers and a flotilla of destroyers should have been routed and put to flight with severe torpedo and gunfire injury, in broad daylight, by a force of five British light cruisers and destroyers, constitutes a naval episode of the highest distinction and entitles all ranks and ratings concerned, and above all their commander, to the compliments of the British nation.

Winston S. Churchill.

Ships taking part:

Rear-Admiral P. L. Vian, DSO, Commanding 15th Cruiser Squadron

HMS *Cleopatra*	Captain G. Grantham, DSO, RN
HMS *Euryalus*	Captain E. W. Bush, DSO, DSC, RN
HMS *Dido*	Captain H. W. U. McCall, RN
HMS *Carlisle*	Captain D. M. L. Neame, DSO, RN
HMS *Penelope*	Captain A. D. Nicholl, DSO, RN

14th Destroyer Flotilla, Captain A. L. Poland, DSO, DSC, RN

22nd Destroyer Flotilla, Captain St J. A. Micklethwait, DSO, RN

Cunningham's prestige was so great that the imminence of his departure had to be kept secret from the enemy. At his going, however, he sent a message to Malta stressing the continuing importance of the island's offensive role against enemy shipping. Though unable any longer to maintain surface ships, they could still play their part in enduring the ceaseless battering suffered by the fortress. In the meantime submarines and torpedo bombers must continue their offensive. Nevertheless Malta's sufferings were increasing, as evidenced by the ruins and mounting rubble, and the diminishing rations of vital food and drinking water for the populace. Moreover, for three months the enemy had been sending supplies in increasing quantities to Tripoli and Benghazi with only occasional interference by British forces. And any such interruption was now falling off markedly.

Malta could not survive without supplies, and the prospect of sending further convoys could be envisaged only if fighter defence were greatly increased. Similarly the need to frustrate the increasing air assault stemming from Sicily, could only be satisfied by the allocation of British bombers for the purpose; bombers which could also attack Tripoli and Italian ports as well, and the airfields in Sardinia that provided such a hazard for the aircraft carriers bringing fighters to Malta from the United Kingdom.

Germany was being heavily attacked at this time by bombers based in England, and the reigning policy deplored any reduction of such an offensive that might result from the sending of bombers to the Mediterranean.

The position in the Western Desert on which Malta's future security so much depended was almost a stalemate. By the end of April 1942 Malta had become for all practicable purposes neutralised, the remains of the 10th Submarine Flotilla continuing with the greatest difficulty, and the RAF bombers and FAA torpedo bombers so low in strength as to be almost impotent in spite of gallant sorties. This was the moment of Malta's greatest trial.

Recognition and encouragement however came on April 15th with a message from HM King George VI:

"To honour her brave people I award the George Cross to the Island fortress of Malta to bear witness to a heroism and devotion that will long be famous in history."

Miraculously it seemed, within a few days, their fortitude was rewarded in a more practical way by the sudden falling off of German Luftwaffe attacks after April 28th. This was due to the transfer of German aircraft to the Russian front, and although Italian bombers appeared regularly, attacks were less persistent. This marked the end of Malta's most acute stage of hardship during which in April alone 6,700 tons of bombs were dropped, almost half in the dockyard area, and not much less on the airfields.

No relief was immediately in sight however in the shape of supplies, though the hard won cargo surviving from convoy MW 10 still helped a little to sustain the meagre rations of so many commodities.

The Chiefs of Staff in London had on April 23rd announced that no convoy could be run to Malta in May, either from the west or from the east, as the providential escape of the March convoy, "which was mainly due to the weather", they said, was unlikely to be repeated, if — as was probable — the Italian fleet challenged in strength. Whilst such a phrase sounded somewhat ungracious after Vian's bold and brilliant performance at Sirte, the facts could not be ignored. Neither capital ships nor aircraft carriers could be spared for such a hazardous occupation at the moment, because of operations that were imminent in the Indian Ocean.

Some alleviation appeared likely when 47 Spitfires were flown off the United States carrier *Wasp* on April 20th, from the west, and all but one reached Malta. Regrettably they suffered severely both in the air and on the ground from fighters and bombers sent over from Sicily to destroy them.

Thanks to the generosity of the American President the *Wasp* was made available for a further effort, and on the night of May 7th she was joined off Gibraltar by the British carrier *Eagle.* An escort comprising the *Renown, Charybdis, Cairo* and destroyers steamed eastward with the two carriers to a suitable flying off position about 60 miles north of Algiers, and on May 9th, 64 Spitfires were flown off, of which 60 arrived safely in Malta. This time arrangements had been made to receive, refuel, and rearm the fighters immediately on arrival, and they were more than ready to greet enemy aircraft when they attacked.

Moreover, the fast minelayer *Welshman* disguised as a French destroyer, and carrying stores and ammunition, went through with the carriers, and then on to Malta at high speed to disembark her cargo and begin her return journey westward to rejoin the carriers. She remained but seven hours in Malta, and her disembarkation was greatly assisted by the new Spitfires who shot down numerous enemy aircraft on both May 9th and May 10th. Daylight raiding was brought to an abrupt end on May 10th.

A further batch of 17 Spitfires were flown in from the *Eagle,* on May 18th, and local air superiority by the British was now assured over Malta. The tide had turned.

The fate of Malta was, however, still in the balance after her air victories of May 9th and 10th, and her stocks of food and vital supplies more slender than ever. There was no immediate prospect of any alleviation. The Axis plan to take Malta had not been cancelled. It was merely in abeyance, pending a promising result from Rommel's imminent offensive in the Western Desert. This began May 26th, 1942, and though at first he was held by stubborn British resistance, Rommel had taken Tobruk by June 21st; and before the end of June was at El Alamein, less than 60 miles from Alexandria.

This Axis success led to a further postponement of their intention to invade Malta, for the capture of Alexandria was now in sight. But General Auchinleck defeated Rommel's attempt to break the Allied line at El Alamein in early July, and there he decided to stand fast, building forces, armour, and equipment. Malta in the meantime had received further aircraft reinforcements and was once again in a position to resume her offensive against Axis supply routes, by surface ships, strike aircraft, and submarine, thus assisting the build-up of the Eighth Army.

Bragadin (p 169) says: "The decision to postpone the assault on Malta constituted the most serious, and certainly the most fatal, error of the whole Mediterranean war. It certainly marked the downward path of Axis fortune in the Mediterranean. The air forces in Malta were built up with great rapidity . . . and Malta unsheathed again its 'flaming sword'. THE SUPPLY LINES TO LIBYA WERE AGAIN PLACED IN A STRANGLEHOLD."

It would be wrong to say that Malta's survival was due to Vian's victory at the Second Battle of Sirte, but it is fairly certain that if he had been defeated and the convoy completely destroyed on Passion Sunday, that Malta must soon have been compelled to surrender through sheer necessity.

In the event she survived her supreme test of endurance and lived to play a vital part in the struggle which was to end in victory for the Allies.

CHAPTER FOURTEEN

Memoir

Admiral of the Fleet Sir Philip Vian,
GCB, KBE, DSO.

Philip Vian began his naval career as a cadet at Osborne in May 1907, and passed out from Dartmouth in 1911. He served at the Battle of Jutland in a destroyer, later specialised in gunnery, and spent the first two years of World War II as Captain (D) of the 4th Destroyer Flotilla. It was as captain of the *Cossack* that he became famous when he took that destroyer into the Josing Fiord in Norway to rescue 200 British seamen imprisoned in the German raider *Altmark*.

Promoted Rear-Admiral July 1941, after only 6½ years as a captain, he was given command of the 15th Cruiser Squadron in the Mediterranean in October 1941, and became distinguished for his boldness and skill in action against great odds.

In 1943 he had his first experience of Combined Operations when he commanded one of the three British Assault Forces at the landings in Sicily. At Salerno in the same year, he commanded a squadron of aircraft carriers.

Vian took command of the whole of the British naval forces under Admiral Sir Bertram Ramsay for the landings in Normandy June 1944, and followed this as Commander of the Aircraft Carrier Squadron in the British Pacific Fleet in 1945.

In peace he held successively the appointments of Fifth Sea Lord, and Commander-in-Chief Home Fleet; and in June 1952 he was promoted Admiral of the Fleet for outstanding service.

Shortly after Vian's death in May, 1968, Admiral Sir Henry McCall, KCVO, KBE, CB, DSO, who supported him so closely in the *Dido* during the whole of that brilliant action in the Gulf of Sirte on Passion Sunday, March 22nd, 1942, and who probably knew him better than any of his contemporaries, wrote the following note:

"With the death of Philip Vian we part with one of our great fighting admirals of the school of Andrew Cunningham. The country owes him much. No other senior naval officer was so constantly in action against the enemy during the whole of Hitler's war:

  (a) In the early part as Captain of Destroyers in the North sea, Western Approaches, and North Russia, in which period he gained the DSO and two bars.
  (b) In the Eastern Mediterranean until 1942 as a specially promoted Rear-Admiral. (He was knighted for his action over the Italians off Sirte).
  (c) In command of Force V at the invasion of Sicily.
  (d) In command of the British Naval Forces at the invasion of Normandy.
  (e) For the last two years of the war in command of Aircraft Carriers in the Pacific.

"Those in closest contact with him realised most clearly his great qualities of leadership; his quick appraisement of a situation; clear decisive orders; unhesitating acceptance of responsibility; and willingness to delegate it when the occasion demanded. Those under him knew exactly where they stood, and that they would invariably have his backing.

"I count myself fortunate to have served with him between the wars, and under him during the war. Our friendship which continued into the years of retirement is one that I have prized greatly.

"Those who did not know him well were surprised by the self effacement that runs through his book of his life at sea, *Action This Day*, for he demanded much of his subordinates, and at times could be exacting. But as so often the case with a great character, he was fundamentally simple, thoughtful and kindly."

Principal Commanders

British
Commander-in-Chief Mediterranean: Admiral Sir Andrew Cunningham (HQ in Alexandria)
Commander-in-Chief Middle East: General Sir Claude Auchinleck (HQ in Cairo)
Air Officer Commander-in-Chief: Air Marshal A. W. Tedder (HQ in Cairo)
Rear Admiral 15th Cruiser Squadron: Rear-Admiral Philip Vian (Flag in *Cleopatra*)

Note:
Names of Commanding Officers are on pp 17–18; and in Appendix B. Names of Divisional Leaders in Vian's Striking Force are on pp 22–23

Italian
Commander-in-Chief Italian Fleet: Admiral Angelo Iachino (Flag in *Littorio*)
Admiral of 3rd Cruiser Division: Admiral Parona (Flag in *Gorizia*)

Note:
The Italian Commander-in-Chief Admiral Iachino, born in 1890, and now living in Rome, was Italian Naval Attache in London 1931–1934. His specialist field was gunnery in which he became an outstanding expert. His ability to reach a quick decision made him a good leader much liked by all those who served under him.

British Warships at Battle of Sirte

(a)   Cruisers
Arethusa Class, Dido Class, and Capetown Class

(i)   Arethusa class
Penelope:
Captain A. D. Nicholl, DSO; (of Malta's Force K) 5,270 tons, 32¼ knots, six 6in, eight 4in AA
Completed at Harland & Wolff 1935; lost Feb 18th, 1944

Additional Armament: eight 2pdr AA, eight 0.5in, six 21in TT (Torpedo Tubes)
Propulsion: 4-shaft geared turbines SHP 64,000 = 32¼ knots
Complement: 450
Protection: main belt 2in, deck 2in, turrets 1in, DCT 1in
Dimensions: length 506ft (overall), beam 51ft, draught 13¾ft
Radar: 281, 284, and 285

(ii)   Dido class
Dido:
Captain H. W. U. McCall
Completed at Cammell Laird 1939; scrapped 1958

Cleopatra:
Captain G. Grantham, DSO, (flag of Rear Admiral P. Vian, DSO)
Completed at Hawthorn Leslie 1940; scrapped 1958

Euryalus:
Captain E. W. Bush, DSO, DSC
Completed at Hawthorn Leslie 1939; scrapped 1959

5,450 tons, 33 knots, ten 5.25in (except *Dido,* eight 5.25in and one 4in AA)

Additional Armament: eight 2pdr AA, eight 0.5in, six 21in TT
Propulsion: 4-shaft geared turbines SHP 62,000 = 33 knots
Complement: 550
Protection: main belt 3in, deck 2in, turrets 2in, DCT 1in
Dimensions: length 512ft (overall), beam 50ft, draught 14ft
Radar: 281 and 285 (except *Euryalus* 279, 284, 285, and 282)

(iii)   **Capetown class**
Carlisle:
Captain D. M. L. Neame, DSO
4,290 tons, 29 knots, eight 4in AA, four 2pdr, eight 0.5in
Completed at Fairfield 1918; converted to AA Cruiser; scrapped 1949
Propulsion: 2-shaft geared turbines SHP 40,000 = 29 knots
Complement: 400
Protection: main belt 3in, deck 1in, CT 3in
Dimensions: length 452ft (overall), beam 43½ft, draught 14¼ft
Radar: 280 (warning and fire control)

(b)   **Destroyers**
H Class, Tribal Class, J Class, K Class, L Class, and Hunt Class

(i)   **H class**
Hero 22nd DF:
Commander R. L. Fisher, DSO, OBE
Completed on the Tyne 1936; transferred to RCN, 1943

Havock 22nd DF:
Lt-Cdr G. R. G. Watkins, DSC
Completed at Derry 1936; lost April 6th, 1942

Hasty 22nd DF:
Lt-Cdr N. H. G. Austen

Completed at Derry 1936; lost June 15th, 1942
1,340 tons, 36 knots, four 4.7in, eight 0.5in, eight 21in TT, (except *Havock,* four TT and one 3in)
Propulsion: 2-shaft geared turbines SHP 34,000 = 36 knots
Complement: 145
Protection: Nil
Dimensions: length 323ft (overall), beam 32¼ft, draught 8½ft
Radar: 286 (except *Hero* nil)

(ii)   Tribal class
Sikh 22nd DF:
Captain St J. A. Micklethwait, DSO
Completed at Stephen 1937; lost September 14th, 1942

Zulu 22nd DF:
Commander H. R. Graham, DSO, DSC
Completed at Stephen 1937; lost September 14th, 1942

1,870 tons, 36 knots, six 4.7in, two 4in AA, four 21in TT
AA Armament: also four 2pdr and eight 0.5in
Propulsion: 2-shaft geared turbines SHP 44,000 = 36 knots
Complement: 190
Protection: Nil
Dimensions: length 378ft (overall), beam 36½ft, draught 9ft
Radar: 286

(iii)   J class and K class
Jervis 14th DF:
Captain A. L. Poland, DSO, DSC
Completed at Hawthorn Leslie 1938; scrapped 1949

1,760 tons, 36 knots, six 4.7in, nine 21in TT

AA Armament: also four 2pdr and eight 0.5in
Propulsion: 2-shaft geared turbines SHP 40,000 = 36 knots
Complement: 218
Protection: Nil
Dimensions: length 357ft (overall), beam 36ft, draught 9ft
Radar: 286

Kipling 14th DF:
Commander A. St Clair-Ford, DSO
Completed at Yarrow 1939; lost May 11th, 1942
As for *Jervis,* but also one 4in AA and only five TT

Kelvin 14th DF:
Commander J. H. Allison, DSO
Completed at Fairfield 1939; scrapped June 1949
As for *Kipling*

Kingston 14th DF:
Commander P. Somerville, DSO, DSC
Completed at White 1939; lost April 11th, 1942
As for *Kipling*

Note:
Tripod foremast, no main mast, single funnel, only two
boilers: typical of the Js and Ks

(iv) L class
Lively 22nd DF:
Lt-Cdr W. F. E. Hussey, DSO
Completed Cammell Laird 1941; lost May 11th, 1942

Legion Force K, Malta:
Commander R. F. Jessel
Completed Hawthorn Leslie 1940; lost March 25th, 1942

1,920 tons, 36 knots, eight 4in AA, eight 21in TT

AA Armament: also four 2pdr, two 20mm, eight 0.5in
Propulsion: 2-shaft geared turbines SHP 48,000 = 36 knots
Complement: 226
Protection: Nil
Dimensions: length 363ft (overall), beam 37ft, draught 10ft
Radar: 285 and 286

Note:
Full torpedo armament of eight TT, and eight 4in guns in twin
fully enclosed mountings.

103

(v)   Hunt class Escort Destroyers of 5th DF:
(Completed 1940–41)
Southwold:
Commander C. T. Jellicoe, DSC; lost March 24th, 1942
Beaufort:
Lt-Cdr Sir O. G. Roche, Bart; transferred RNN 1954
Dulverton:
Lt-Cdr W. N. Petch, OBE; lost November 13th, 1943
Hurworth:
Lt-Cdr J. T. B. Birch; lost October 22nd, 1943
Avon Vale:
Lt-Cdr P. A. R. Withers, DSC; scrapped 1958
Eridge:
Lt-Cdr W. F. N. Gregory Smith, DSC; disabled August 29th, 1942
Heythrop:
Lt-Cdr R. S. Stafford; lost March 20th, 1942

1,050 tons, 25 knots, six 4in AA, no torpedoes

AA Armament: also four 2pdr and two 20mm
Propulsion: 2-shaft geared turbines SHP 19,000 = 25 knots
Complement: 168
Protection: Nil
Dimensions: length 283ft (overall), beam 31½ft, draught 8ft
Radar: 285 and 286

(c)   **Submarines**
U class (completed 1940–41) and P class

(i)   U class
Unbeaten:
Lt-Cdr E. A. Woodward, DSO; lost November 11th, 1942
P34:
Lt P. R. Harrison, DSC; scrapped 1949
Upholder:
Lt-Cdr M. D. Wanklyn, VC, DSO; lost April 14th, 1942
P36:
Lt H. N. Edmunds, DSC; lost March 31st, 1942

104

545/740 tons, 11¼/9 knots, four TT, one 3in gun

Propulsion: 2-shaft diesel-electric
Complement: 31
Dimensions: length 197ft (overall), beam 16ft, draught 13ft

(ii) P class
Proteus:
Lt-Cdr P. S. Francis; completed 1929, scrapped 1946

1,475/2,040 tons, 17½/9 knots, eight TT, (six in bow, two in stern), one 4in gun

Propulsion: 2-shaft diesel electric
Complement: 53
Dimensions: length 290ft overall, beam 30ft, draught 14ft

Convoy MW 10
HMS *Breconshire*
(10,000 tons) was a commissioned auxiliary supply ship, built and requisitioned in 1939; and commanded by the Commodore of the Convoy, Captain C. A. G. Hutchinson, DSO. She was disabled March 23rd, damaged again March 26th, and finally sank in Marsa Xlokk March 27th, 1942
Clan Campbell
(17,500 tons) was sunk off Malta, March 23rd, 1942
Pampas
(15,500 tons) was sunk at Malta, March 26th 1942
Talabot (Norwegian)
(17,500 tons) was sunk at Malta, March 26th, 1942

Italian Warships at the Battle of Sirte

(a)   **Battleships**
(i)   *Littorio*
(Flag of Admiral Iachino)
46,000 tons (full load), 28 knots (wartime best speed), nine
15in guns (max range 32 sea miles)
Completed 1940; renamed *Italia* July 1943; surrendered to
Cunningham September 10th, 1943; scrapped at La Spezia
1948

Additional Armament: twelve 6in (max range 13½ sea miles),
twelve 3.5in AA, four 4.7in, twenty 37mm, thirty 20mm
Aircraft: Three float planes
Propulsion: 4-shaft geared turbines, SHP 130,000 = 28 knots
Complement: 1,872
Protection: side 350mm, deck 207, CT 260, turrets 150–350
Dimensions: length 237.76m, beam 32.92m, draught 9.58m

(b)   **Heavy Cruisers:**
(i)   *Zara class*
Gorizia
(Flag of Admiral Parona)
14,600 tons (full load), 29 knots (wartime best speed), eight
8in (max range 17 sea miles)
Completed 1931 at Trieste, scuttled at La Spezia September
8th, 1943, seized by Germans and later sunk by Italo-British
human torpedoes June 1944 at La Spezia

Additional Armament: sixteen 3.9in, eight 37mm, and eight
13.2mm. Equipped for two float planes. No torpedoes
Propulsion: 2-shaft geared turbines, SHP 95,000 to 122,000 =
32 knots (designed), and 29 knots, (in practice)

Complement: 830
Protection: side 150mm, deck 70mm, CT 150mm, turrets 150mm
Dimensions: length 183m (overall), beam 20.6m, draught 5.9m

(ii)   *Trento class*
Trento
13,540 tons (full load), 31 knots (wartime best speed), eight 8in (max range 15 sea miles)
Completed 1929 at Leghorn, torpedoed and sunk by HM Submarine *Umbra* June 15th, 1942

Additional Armament: sixteen 3.9in, eight 37mm, and eight 13.2mm; equipped for 3 float planes; eight TT
Propulsion: 4-shaft geared turbines, SHP 150,000 = 31 knots
Complement: 781
Protection: side 75mm, deck 50, CT 100, HC 100
Dimensions: length 197m (overall), beam 20.6m, draught 5.9m

(c)   **Light Cruisers:**
(i)   *Condottieri class*
Bande Nere
7,000 tons (full load), 30 knots (best wartime speed), eight 6in (max range 12 sea miles)
Completed at Castellammare 1931; torpedoed and sunk by HM Submarine *Urge* April 1st, 1942, shortly after the Second Battle of Sirte

Additional Armament: six 3.9in, eight 37mm, eight 13.2mm, four TT, two float planes, equipped for minelaying
Propulsion: 2-shaft geared turbines SHP 124,000 = 30 knots
Complement: 521
Protection: side 25mm, deck 20, CT 40, HC turrets 25
Dimensions: length 169m, beam 15.5m, draught 4.9m

(d)   **Destroyers**
(i)   *Soldati class*
Ascari
Completed at Leghorn 1939; mined March 24th, 1943

Aviere
Completed at Leghorn 1938; sunk by HM Submarine *Splendid* December 17th, 1942
Alpino
Completed at Ancona 1939; bombed and sunk at La Spezia April 19th, 1943
Bersagliere
Completed at Palermo 1939; bombed and sunk at Palermo January 7th, 1943
Fuciliere
Completed at Ancona 1939; transferred to Soviet Russia 1950
Lanciere
Completed at Riva Trigoso 1939; sank in a storm March 23rd, 1942
2,459 tons (full load), 34 knots (best wartime speed), five 4.7in

Additional Armament: one 37mm, eight 20mm, two DCT, six 21in TT. Fitted for minelaying (48)
Propulsion: 2-shaft geared turbines SHP 56,200 = 34 knots
Complement: 219
Dimensions: length 107m, beam 10.15m, draught 3.58m

(ii)   Oriani class
Oriani
Completed at Leghorn 1937; fought at Matapan; transferred to France
2,290 tons (full load), 33 knots (best war time speed), four 4.7in

Additional Armament: two 37mm, eight 20mm, six 21in TT, 2–4 DCT; fitted for minelaying (56)
Propulsion: 2-shaft geared turbines, SHP 55,000 = 33 knots
Complement: 207
Dimensions: length 107m, beam 10.15m, draught 3.42m

(iii)   *Maestrale class*
Grecale
Completed at Ancona 1934; engine broke down at Sirte; she was detached from *Littorio;* rebuilt several times after the end of the war

2,243 tons (full load), 32 knots (best wartime speed), four 4.7in
Additional Armament: eight 20mm, two 13.2mm, six 21in TT, 4 DCT
Propulsion: 2-shaft geared turbines, SHP 50,000 = 32 knots
Complement: 191
Dimensions: length 107m, beam 10.15m, draught 3.31m

Note:
The destroyer *Scirocco* of the Maestrale Class was not in the battle, but was sent from Taranto to join the *Littorio* on March 22nd, 1942, and, like the *Lanciere,* foundered in the violent storm the next morning.

APPENDIX D

Chronology of Main Events Before and After the Battle of Sirte

1941	Nov	13th	Loss of *Ark Royal* after reinforcing Malta's aircraft
		18th	CRUSADER (the 'winter battle') begins with Brish push
		25th	Loss of *Barham*
			Besieged Tobruk continues to be supplied by Inshore Squadron
	Dec	1st	British attempt to relieve Tobruk
		10th	Tobruk relieved
		14th	Loss of *Galatea*
		17th	First Battle of Sirte
		19th	*Queen Elizabeth* and *Valiant* disabled at Alexandria
		25th	British troops enter Benghazi. Fliegerkorps II ordered from Russia to Sicily

1942	Jan	2nd	Bardia falls to the British
		17th	Sollum and Halfaya fall to the British
		21st	Rommel begins counter-offensive
		28th	British withdraw from Benghazi
			Only 3 small convoys reach Malta from Alex during month
	Feb	2nd	British 8th Army at Gazala. No British airfield now closer than 500 miles from Malta
		15th	British convoy from Alex fails to reach Malta
	Mar	11th	Loss of *Naiad*
		22nd	Second Battle of Sirte
		23rd	British convoy reaches Malta, only to be destroyed by Axis bombing
			Lull in the desert continues. Air attacks on Malta continue
	Apr	15th	George Cross awarded to Malta
		20th	USS *Wasp* flies Spitfires into Malta
			Both sides preparing for major operations in desert. Malta is soon to face her supreme trial
	May	9th	*Wasp* and *Eagle* fly in more Spitfires to Malta
		10th	British War Cabinet order Auchinleck to attack this month
		10th	Axis aircraft severely defeated in battles over Malta
		18th	*Eagle* flies in more Spitfires to Malta, and though the position is still precarious the tide is about to turn later this year
		26th	Rommel however forestalls Auchinleck and attacks Gazala

Gunnery Aspect

The remarkable aspect of this battle in which four light cruisers and 11 destroyers under Vian, had held at bay a modern battleship, three cruisers, and seven destroyers for two and a half hours, is that there should have been such relatively little damage and loss. The offensive was nearly always with Vian, who was greatly helped by his use of smoke for screening purposes, and also by the fact that he was able to maintain the windward gauge from start to finish, and thus maintain the initiative, and at the same time prevent Iachino's fleet from sighting the convoy.

The Italians received a few hits from the British 6in, 5.25in, 4.7in and 4in guns, mostly on the battleship which was frequently straddled but suffered no vital damage. Nor did the British ships suffer, other than the *Cleopatra,* unfortunate in sustaining several casualties when hit by a 6in shell from the *Bande Nere* at 16.43; the *Euryalus,* hit by a splinter from one of the *Littorio's* 15in shells shortly afterwards; the *Havock* damaged at 17.20 by a near miss from one of the *Littorio's* 15in shells, which flooded a boiler room and caused casualties; the *Kingston* by a 15in shell as she was about to fire torpedoes at 18.41; and finally the *Lively* damaged at the water line by a 15in splinter at 18.55 when she fired all eight torpedoes at the retiring battleship.

The Italians were overawed by Vian's offensive tactics and the ever present possibility of a sudden torpedo attack from some part of Vian's force emerging from behind the smoke screen. The reason for the relatively ineffectual gunfire on both sides was the long range at which most of the action was fought. There was also the difficulty of observing an identifying fall of shot because of smoke and sea spray, and also the unpredictability of the moment when a target might suddenly appear or disappear.

It was for this reason that Vian chose to close the Italians, giving his force a chance of using their guns to good effect, in addition to providing a constant threat of torpedo attack. The leader of each division would obviously have his view of the Italian ships less obscured than the view from the ships immediately following. This is borne out in some of the individual remarks recorded in the narrative, indicating that close followers were seldom clear of smoke and could see little of what was going on; sometimes in fact having the greatest difficulty in following the movements of the next ahead. The advantage of being in the lead and able thereby to fire more ammunition, is strikingly revealed in the table below, which records the ammunition expended by individual British ships.

Division	Ship	Rounds	Calibre
4	Cleopatra	868	a
	Euryalus	421	a
2	Dido	200	a
	Penelope	64	b
3	Zulu	0	c
	Hasty	4	c
	Sikh	450	c
	Lively	275	d
5	Hero	88	c
	Havock	92	c
	Jervis	106	c
	Kipling	110	c
1	Kelvin	73	c
	Kingston	56	c
	Legion	x	d

legend: x unrecorded; a = 5.2in; b = 6in; c = 4.7in; d = 4in

It is of interest that the pattern of the figures for the British cruisers is, strangely enough, roughly in inverse geometric progression, in spite of the random behaviour of the smoke.

It is obvious that the long range would favour the Italians. The battleship's 15in guns could elevate to 35° if required, thus giving a maximum range of 23 nautical miles; and even her 6in guns had a range of 13 nautical miles, which exceeded the range of the *Penelope's* 6in guns (12 miles) and the *Dido* class 5.25in guns (11½ miles). Except for the *Lively* and *Legion,* both of which had the new 4in HA gun, with a range of 10 miles or more, Vian's remaining destroyers were armed with 4.7in guns whose maximum elevation was only 40° and the range barely 8½ miles.

The expenditure for the Italian ships was as follows:

	15in	8in	6in	4.7in	4in	3.5in
Littorio	181	—	445	—	—	21
Gorizia	—	226	—	—	67	—
Trento	—	355	—	—	20	—
Bande Nere	—	—	112	—	—	—
Aviere	—	—	—	84	—	—
Ascari	—	—	—	0	—	—
Oriani	—	—	—	0	—	—
Alpino	—	—	—	0	—	—
Bersagliere	—	—	—	0	—	—
Fuciliere	—	—	—	0	—	—
Lanciere	—	—	—	0	—	—
TOTAL	181	581	557	84	87	21

The Italian totals compared with the following British totals, indicate a considerably greater rate of fire on the part of Vian's striking force.

British Ships' Totals	6in	5.25in	4.7in	4in
	64	1489	979	257

British Gun Ranges

Official statistics for the maximum range of British guns are as follows, but it should be borne in mind that the higher figures are extremes and are very optimistic. For the purposes of comparison as applied to the Sirte action, the lower figure should be accepted.

Calibre (inches)	Range (yards)	Elevation	Rounds per minutes per gun
6	24,200 to 26,000	60°	6
5.25	23,400 to 26,000	70°	10
4.7	16,800 to 23,000	40°	12
4	19,400 to 20,100	80°	12

APPENDIX F

Close Escort

Air attacks on Vian's covering force and the convoy and escort began at about 09.30 on Sunday March 22nd by which time the radius of action was too great for any protection from British fighters based in Egypt. This was just half an hour after the last fighter patrol had to leave the convoy to return to base. Air attacks were now to continue at intervals for the rest of this Sunday until dark, and it was estimated that 150 aircraft were employed in torpedo attacks, bombing attacks, and in shadowing. The forenoon attacks were not very dangerous, and all enemy torpedoes were eluded.

From 14.45, however, soon after the Italian cruisers had been sighted, attacks from the air were heavy and sustained, and were directed mainly at the convoy until 19.00. Up to 18.00 the air attacks were carried out by formations of three to nine aircraft, almost all German Ju 88s, and thereafter by torpedo aircraft Italian S79s and German He 111s as well.

It was at 14.33 that Vian's divisions turned northwards and then eastwards to lay smoke, and this force included the 6th division, the anti-aircraft cruiser *Carlisle* and the Hunt destroyer *Avon Vale.* This left the convoy under the sole care of the remaining five Hunts, *Southwold* (Commander Jellicoe), *Beaufort, Dulverton, Hurworth,* and *Eridge,* for almost an hour and a half until the *Carlisle* and *Avon Vale* rejoined the convoy at 15.51. The fact that the convoy and escort escaped damage speaks well for the efficacy of these Hunts, as well as for the skilful manoeuvring and shooting by the ships of the convoy. Rear-Admiral Vian remarked that "whilst the striking force was rejoining, the sound of the 4in fire from the Hunts and *Carlisle* was most impressive, resembling continuous pom-pom fire, even though heard at a distance of 8 to 10 miles".

Of the five enemy aircraft known to have been shot down by the close escort and convoy, one each were accounted for by the *Breconshire* and the *Pampas.*

It is interesting to recall that the building of the Hunts was sponsored by Admiral Sir Andrew Cunningham when at the Admiralty as Deputy Chief of Naval Staff 1938–39. He had spent the early years of his naval life almost entirely in destroyers, and was aware that because of the alarming shortage of destroyers that had followed years of disarmament a new design for a small destroyer was required which would allow for rapid building in large numbers. To avoid hurting the susceptibilities of Parliament, the first 20 were included in the Navy estimate as 'escort vessels', rather than 'destroyers'. Originally they were to be 'fast escort vessels', but eventually it was decided to sacrifice speed, as well as radius of action and torpedoes, and concentrate on small vessels equipped with defensive anti-submarine and anti-aircraft armament. The extra speed in fleet destroyers, so expensively obtained in the matter of size and price and lengthy period of building, was not of great use in a submarine hunt if asdic listening became impracticable at the higher speeds. Thus developed the principle that although fast fleet destroyers were essential when in attendance on the fleet, slower vessels such as corvettes could do the work of convoy escort, and be produced more quickly and in greater numbers than the multi-purpose destroyer.

In the case of the Hunts a speed of 25 knots was accepted and an armament of 4in guns with a high-angle control system, and 20mm and 2pdr, but no torpedoes. The displacement was a little over 1,000 tons compared with a figure more than double that amount for the fleet destroyer.

Cunningham says that the Hunts did not entirely come up to expectation for convoy work in the Atlantic. But for general service in the more limited waters like the North Sea, English Channel, and Mediterranean, they were invaluable during World War II, particularly for anti-submarine work.

APPENDIX G

The Torpedo Aspect

The torpedo appears to have been the greatest hazard facing the Italians on this wild day of battle north of the Gulf of Sirte, yet no hits were scored either by those fired from the *Jervis* division or those from the *Sikh* division. In all cases the range was great; moreover the accuracy of setting was markedly affected by the necessity for spontaneity and the intermittent sighting provided by gaps in the drifting smoke. Nevertheless the fact that there were confident claims of hits indicates that the Italians had some narrow escapes from the weapon they most feared. A big reduction of their speed might have been brought about at any minute, and this would have provided opportunities for individual attacks from various directions, the sort of offensive at which Vian showed particular skill, obliging the enemy, in the words of Kempenfelt "to think of nothing but being on guard against your attack".

The surprising feature is not the great range at which torpedoes were fired, but that the British destroyer divisions and Vian's cruisers were able to get as close as they did without serious loss. This was due entirely to the fact that the British maintained the initiative throughout, and the torpedo attacks made by the 1st and 5th divisions were magnificently conducted in spite of rough weather and uncertain visibility in the face of heavy gunfire. It is certain that it was due to the torpedo attacks that the Italian ships turned away and finally withdrew rapidly from the scene as darkness descended.

This raises an interesting point which Commander R. L. Fisher, the captain of the *Hero*, must have had in mind when remarking that he thought he saw the enemy ships turning away and he decided not to waste torpedoes on such a poor target. As previously stated, he was under the impression that there would be much more profitable use for them during the coming night. He had been at Matapan and presumably had memories of the mopping up operations of the fleet destroyers during the night when three heavy Italian cruisers, the *Zara*, *Fiume*, and *Pola*, and two Italian destroyers, the *Alfieri* and *Carducci*, had all been sunk. There were, however, three factors which militated against a continuance of the action after dark:

(a) fuel and ammunition considerations,
(b) the difficulty of identifying friend from foe in the dark in deteriorating weather,
(c) the desirability of getting through as much of Bomb Alley as was possible in the dark.

It may be remarked that each of the cruisers in Vian's striking force was equipped with six torpedo tubes, but only the *Cleopatra* fired, in this case her three starboard torpedoes at 18.06. No hits were seen, and no other cruiser fired, the range being far too great — 6 or 7 miles — and the viewing of the enemy ships only intermittent.

The number of torpedo tubes fitted to Fleet destroyers varied between four and nine, and changes were made long after completion, either by a reduction to compensate for the additional top weight involved in the installation of a new type of gun, or an increase if lighter guns and equipment were installed. The Tribals had only four torpedo tubes, but were succeeded by the smaller Js and Ks in which there were as many (at first) as 10 torpedo tubes. The Ks, (with only two boilers), can be distinguished in the photographs by the single funnel, tripod foremast, and absence of a mainmast. The Ls (in the case of the *Legion* and *Lively*) were fitted with eight of the new 4in AA guns and eight torpedo tubes. In the photographs the above two Ls can be seen to have their guns in pairs in four fully enclosed turrets, but are otherwise distinguishable from the Ks by virtue of the latter having only six 4.7in guns in three pairs.

The small Hunts were slower than the Fleet destroyers and had no torpedo tubes, but were equipped with six 4in anti-aircraft guns.

A record of the torpedoes fired by Captain Micklethwait's 5th division during the battle is not available, but the following table gives details of the 25 fired by Captain Poland's 1st division at about 18.40.

Ships	Torpedoes Fired	Comments from Report
Jervis	5 out of 9	"Owing to difficulty in controlling the swing in the prevailing bad weather, was able to fire only 5 torpedoes"
Kipling	All 5	— —
Kelvin	4 out of 5	"Fired two prematurely at 1835, having mistaken the signal to 'turn to run in' for a signal to 'fire'."
Kingston	3 out of 5	"Two torpedo-tubes damaged by gunfire."
Legion	All 8	— —

Aircraft Background

(a) The Luftwaffe in the Mediterranean

The Luftwaffe first arrived in the Mediterranean in January 1941 with the establishment of Fliegerkorps X in Sicily, with the object of attacking Malta and shipping passing through the narrows between Sicily and Tunis. Units of this body were detached to Libya to support Rommel, but not to come under his orders. Fliegerkorps X also played a part in the capture of Crete. But the operation was mainly carried out by Fliegerkorps VIII and Fliegerkorps XI, of which the former provided the reconnaissance, fighter, and bomber support, while the latter comprised all the airborne troops, gliders, parachutes, transport planes, and craft: in all about 22,000 men.

As soon as Crete was captured the crippled remains of the two Fliegerkorps VIII and XI were withdrawn, and Fliegerkorps X took up station to cover the Aegean and North Africa, with its headquarters in Greece. Aircraft in use were the single-engined dive bombers Ju 87, the long-range bombers Ju 88 and He 111; and the fighters Me 109 and Me 110. Because of the scattered nature of airfields, about 80 Ju 52 transport planes were maintained. Total strength then was of the order of 400, of which only about half were serviceable at any time.

It was in December 1941 that Hitler decided to transfer Fliegerkorps II from the Russian front to Sicily; and with the withdrawal of British troops from Cyrenaica in the face of Rommel's counter-offensive which began January 21st, 1942, Bomb Alley was once again under the domination of the Luftwaffe.

The Axis successes on land were a further heavy blow to Admiral Cunningham who had lost so many ships towards the end of 1941, and was then without either capital ships or aircraft carriers. Nor was there any likelihood of reinforcements in either of these categories, because of the immediate demands in the Indian Ocean and Far East following Japan's entry into the war.

Early in February 1942 he wrote to the First Sea Lord in the following terms: "I am, as I am sure you are, bitterly disappointed at the turn the Libyan Campaign has taken . . . I know it is not due to any naval short-comings. We had just landed over 2,500 tons of petrol and over 3,000 tons of other stores at Benghazi, and had doubled the amount we had guaranteed to land daily at Tobruk . . . I have pressed on the Commander-in-Chief Middle East Forces, the necessity of holding a line as far forward as possible . . . I am alarmed about Malta's supplies.

"If we could hold as far forward as Derna I believe we could supply Malta from Alexandria, but we are already behind that line."

Malta to Derna is a distance of 530 miles.

It became all too clear that without adequate fighter defence in Malta, and with no British airfields in North Africa as far west as Derna, and in the absence of an aircraft carrier, the possibility of getting merchant ships from Alexandria to Malta was going to become less likely than ever, since the radius of action would be too great.

There was nothing new in Cunningham's appeal for more air support and the holding of territory essential for its strategic use.

(b) The Need for Aircraft Carriers

After the battle for Crete in May 1941, Cunningham wrote "The struggle in no way proved that the air is master over the sea. The proper way to fight the air is in the air." He warned that there should be no hasty conclusion that ships are impotent in the face of air attack. The presence of a few RAF fighters, when they were able to attend Cunningham's ships in the last few days of the evacuation from Crete, made a considerable difference, and permitted the ships in some cases to complete their passage unhindered. Cunningham would, however, have been content with a modern aircraft carrier armed with a full complement of serviceable fighters and bombers. By virtue of their design for fleet use, the carrier-based aircraft were unlikely to match the performance of shore-based aircraft, but the great advantage was that they were flown by naval men who were familiar with ships and the sea, and moreover were under the naval Commander-in-Chief's complete control.

In the event, Cunningham in 1941 and 1942, was more often without either carrier-based or shore-based aircraft. Prewar policy for defence in certain areas had worked on the assumption that the fleet and shipping would not be far from certain shore bases from which aircraft could provide protection. In the Royal Navy itself there had been, between the wars, a degree of apathy towards 'air', and as late as 1940 there were still many naval officers who regarded the battleship as the primary unit of strength. In their eyes all other units existed for roles complementary to the paramount importance of the big ship.

In spite of setbacks suffered by the Fleet Air Arm of the Royal Navy during the years 1918 to 1937, whilst removed from the effectual control of the Admiralty, that Arm made a remarkable recovery from 1937 onwards, growing from a small force into a weapon whose full potential of patrol, reconnaissance, offence, and defence in a fleet action was first realised at Matapan. Taranto, a few months earlier, had demonstrated also the great offensive potential of this long-range weapon launched from a mobile base providing the indispensable strategical and tactical factors of flexibility and surprise.

The lessons were not lost on the Japanese, who were to have their own Taranto at Pearl Harbour before 1941 was ended. Nor were they lost on the Italians, but it was already too late for them to do anything effectual. Britain was pitifully weak in the number of modern carriers she possessed, and in aircraft and airmen to operate them; the carrier was always singled out for destruction and became the centre and prime target of enemy attacks. Britain began the war with a collection of vulnerable carriers, the old *Argus, Eagle, Hermes, Courageous, Glorious, Furious,* and the new *Ark Royal.* Of these only the *Argus* and *Furious* survived the war.

Thanks to the foresight of a former First Sea Lord, Lord Chatfield, six carriers with armoured flight deck were on order at the outbreak of war. *Illustrious* became operational by

August 1940, *Formidable* by November 1940, *Victorious* by May 1941, *Indomitable* by December 1941, *Indefatigable* by July 1944, and *Implacable* by October 1944. Had we received them a year or two earlier, those tragic losses in the Mediterranean in 1941 and 1942 would probably not have happened.

A succession of escort carriers (as well as new aircraft) continued to flow in later years from the USA for the Royal Navy, with such aggressive names as *Attacker, Biter, Chaser, Dasher, Fencer, Hunter, Pursuer, Striker,* followed by the Ruler Class of carriers. These were to play a great role of flexible and swift support exactly where required most. Without them our seaborne landings in the various spheres in the Mediterranean Sea in 1943 must have failed, especially those distant from shore bases. The Italian Air Force had the ear of Mussolini who supported their wish for independence from the Army and the Navy (as existed in Germany), and were justly proud of their competence in high level bombing.

This independence led, however, to a lack of understanding of naval requirements by the air force, and a failure to develop the aerial torpedo to any great extent, which the British Fleet Air Arm made such a formidable and effectual weapon, threatening even the heaviest and best protected battleships. Meanwhile the Germans continued to develop their deadly dive-bombing technique. The arrival of Spitfires at Malta in March, April, and May 1942 of course turned the tide. Until then a few Hurricanes had to suffice. In normal times these were found to be more than a match for Italian types in performance, and they could outmanoeuvre the Me 110. But they lacked range.

Italian aircraft generally compared favourably with German or British counterparts in 1941 and 1942, as can be seen in the tables in the next section. What must be remembered is that until the latter half of 1942, long after Sirte, the total of Italian and German air strength was overwhelmingly greater than that which the British could muster in the Mediterranean.

(c) *Relative Performance of Aircraft*
The figures given in the tables below may serve as a useful guide in the matter of the limiting radius of action. They

provide only a general guide, and it must be realised that they will vary with such factors as climate, wind, loading, altitude, extra tanks (LRT), and accuracy of navigation. This applies especially to what I have termed the Endurance Range, ie the distance that can be flown in still air until the tanks are empty. Endurance Range must not be confused with Radius of Action.

In view of the fact that distances over the sea are quoted in sea miles, all the endurance ranges are given in sea miles. (One sea mile equals 2,000 yards equals 1 1/7 statute miles. Hence 7 sea miles = 8 statute miles).

For a similar reason all speeds are quoted in knots.

$$(7 \text{ knots} = \frac{8 \text{ statute miles}}{\text{hour}}$$

Relative Performance of Aircraft (Fighters)

Type	Armament	Crew	Fuel (gallons)	Economical Speed (knots)	Maximum Speed (knots)	Endurance Range (sea miles)	Nationality
Beaufighter Twin Engine monoplane	6 x .303 4 x 20mm	2	550	200 at 15,000ft	287 at 11,750ft	1,335	British–RAF
Hurricane I Single Engine monoplane	8 x .303	1	97	160 at 15,000ft	280 at 17,750ft	528	British–RAF
Spitfire VB Single Engine monoplane	4 x .303 2 x 20mm	1	85	182 at 20,000ft	328 at 20,250ft	420	British–RAF
Me 109 F Single Engine monoplane	2 x 7.9mm 3 x 20mm	1	88	175 at 17,000ft	346 at 22,000ft	570	German
Me 110 Twin Engine monoplane	6 x 7.9mm 2 x 20mm	2	280	176 at 18,000ft	317 at 20,000ft	820	German
C.R. 42 Single Engine biplane	2 x 12.7mm	1	535	132 at 13,100ft	238 at 13,100ft	470	Italian

Relative Performance of Aircraft (Bombers)

Type	Armament	Crew	Bomb-load (lbs)	Economical Speed (knots)	Maximum Speed (knots)	Endurance Range (sea miles)	Nationality
Blenheim I Twin Engine monoplane	2 x .303	3	1,000	145 at 15,000ft	234 at 15,000ft	810	British–RAF
Wellington I Twin Engine monoplane	6 x .303	6	1,000 or 4,500	145 at 10,000ft	200 at 4,700ft	2,250 or 1,160	British–RAF
Albacore Single Engine biplane	2 x .303	3 or 2*	1,500 or Torpedo	100 at 6,000ft	144 at 4,800ft	460 or 850*	British–Fleet Air Arm *Use of Long-range Tank
Swordfish Single Engine biplane	2 x .303	2	1,500 or Torpedo	90 at 5,000ft	120 at 5,000ft	465	British–Fleet Air Arm (nicknamed STRINGBAG)
Beaufort II Twin Engine monoplane	4 x .303	4	1,650 or Torpedo	140 at 5,000ft	228 at 14,500ft	1,125	British–RAF
Ju87 (Stuka) Single Engine monoplane	3 x 7.9mm	2	1,100	141 at 15,000ft	216 at 15,000ft	317	German

125

Relative Performance of Aircraft (Bombers)

Type	Armament	Crew	Bomb-load (lbs)	Economical Speed (knots)	Maximum Speed (knots)	Endurance Range (sea miles)	Nationality
Ju 88 Twin Engine monoplane	7 x 7.9mm 1 x 20mm	4	2,200	171 at 16,400ft	260 at 14,000ft	1,150	German
He III Twin Engine monoplane	7 x 7.9mm 2 x 20mm	5 or 6	2,200	159 at 17,000ft	211 at 14,000ft	1,330	German
Ju 52 Three Engine monoplane	5 x 7.9mm	2	5,000 (freight)	116 at sea level	145 at sea level	466 to 695	German
Cant. Z. 506 Three Engine seaplane	1 x 12.7mm 3 x 7.7mm	4 or 5	1,750	123 at 13,000ft	202 at 13,000ft	1,000	Italian
S79 Three Engine monoplane	3 x 12.7mm 2 x 7.7mm	4 or 5	2,750 or Torpedo	137 at 13,000ft	224 at 13,000ft	1,050	Italian

An Engineer's Tale

The engineer officer of the destroyer *Kelvin,* now Rear Admiral I. G. Aylen CB, OBE, DSC, remarks on the fact that she was a happy ship: one of the redoubtable 5th Destroyer Flotilla which had been nurtured from the slip by Captain (D) Lord Louis Mountbatten.

These ships were the first to be fitted operationally with the Mountbatten Station Keeper, an equipment devised by Lord Louis. It allowed the officer of the watch to make minor changes in the ship's position in formation, by ordering an advance or retirement to the engine room in yards rather than by a sudden increase or decrease in revolutions. Though viewed with mixed feelings by bridge watch keepers it certainly found favour among engineer officers as their machinery generally received less drastic treatment, particularly when steaming in line ahead at 25 knots or more which was so favoured by Captain (D).

Mountbatten's exploits became a byword. Each time he transferred his broad black funnel band to another ship in the Flotilla after his heroic doings in *Kelly,* something drastic inevitably happened. But his incredible energy, enthusiasm, and knowledge of those around him bound his flock together. It was therefore a tragic blow to the 5th DF when the Leader *Kelly* and also the *Kashmir* were sunk at Crete, and *Kelvin* was severely damaged aft, involving a long haul to Bombay to rebuild the stern.

By early 1942 *Kelvin* returned in good shape to the Mediterranean to find her position as tense as ever. She was absorbed under a new Leader *Jervis,* D14 (Captain A. L. Poland) with the remaining Js and Ks: but the team spirit of the 5th DF and much of Lord Louis's doctrine persisted. For example, during the time that five of his ships had been 'mined-in' in the Grand Harbour he had sensibly ordered 'abandon ship' at night, so that ships' companies could take shelter during the incessant air attacks, in the underground oil fuel galleries, leaving only a gun's crew and fire party on board.

Similarly after the tragic losses in the *Jersey* which was mined while entering the Grand Harbour, it was a directive that key personnel should be dispersed in action as much as practicable, with the minimum number of men below decks. For instance in a destroyer while the engineer officer was at the engine room throttles, his chief engine room artificer would be visiting the boiler rooms or other machinery spaces, or be at what was known as 'Chiefie's Bridge', a small sheltered space on the iron deck, just forward of the torpedo tubes, and at the top of the engine room hatches through which the engine room telegraphs and controls could be seen. Then the EO and the CERA would change round.

"So it was", writes Aylen, "that on March 22nd, Passion Sunday, I found myself at Action Stations standing at 'Chiefie's Bridge' with the EO's writer, Leading Stoker Martin, that worthy who doubled as the Chief's right hand personal runner, valet, chief clerk, and the privy keeper of the mysteries of the engine room register — an imperturbable character whose loyal support I much valued. Noisy and sporadic firing at single and formations of aircraft had seemed the normal order for some hours.

"Small ships in '42 were not fitted with the efficient broadcasting arrangements which modern ships enjoy enabling all the ship's company to know what goes on. COs were generally well aware of the great importance to morale of keeping the crew informed, but in long tense periods at action stations it was clearly impossible always to tell those between decks what to expect and when. 'Chiefs' normally had a night order book, detailing the overnight instructions to the department. Mine, I fear, was anything but wholly technical, and was used as an information message pad circulated by day or night to the machinery spaces, retailing the latest gossip from the bridge, serious or ribald. It was a constant source of wonder to me that youngsters who until a few months previously had never been to sea so rarely, if ever, cracked under the pretty intense anxiety of action conditions, particularly when confined in the heaving claustrophobic tin box of a machinery space or magazine. For them action stations meant long periods of intense boredom between the sudden shattering explosions of bombs, mines or depth charges, interspersed with one's own gunfire, which though it might be achieving very little always sounded reassuring. I felt therefore that 'Chiefie's Book' as it was called, could help to relieve the tension a little with gossip such as 'Two Heinkels down, one by *Kipling*, great shooting' or *Kelvin* made to D. . .' 'Large black ball floating Green 40; suspect mine' and D. . . replied 'Not mine'."

"I was transfixed as a great water spout shot up ahead of us. I watched it rise and rise, then suddenly as we tore through the water towards it, down it came, tons and tons of it, right on the spot where Martin and I stood. We were washed along the iron deck mercifully into the guard rails, clinging to each other, half over the side, and angrier and wetter than ever. I recollect also thinking I saw exactly what Bunyan had in mind in the valley of the shadow of death, black smoke on one side, white fury and belching gunfire on the other, bombers overhead, submarines underneath, and the incessant barking of our own gunfire."

The amazing fact is that men and material should be able to survive such a condition, and that high morale could rise above it all, as indeed it did.

Range and Endurance

For any operation in the Mediterranean involving destroyers in long distances, an important factor was the fuel endurance range, and as this varied considerably with speed, and also to a smaller extent with the class of destroyer, it was not easily assessable.

Replenishment at sea (RAS) on an adequate scale was impracticable in 1942, though in the previous year, destroyers were frequently provided with oil fuel by the battleships, especially, for example, during the Battle of Crete. With the loss of Crete and Benghazi, British destroyers were more limited in their movements because of the scarcity of suitable fuelling bases, though Tobruk continued to serve as a British supply base during the first half of 1942, before its capture by Rommel in June 1942. In fact the Hunt class vessels put in to Tobruk for refuelling before taking up station as close escort for the March convoy MW 10 destined for Malta.

The problem can be understood more readily by reference to the table relating fuel consumption to speed. As is well known, the rate of fuel consumption increases rapidly with speed. Its efficient use therefore has to be a compromise governed by the necessity for moderate economic speed as opposed to the demand for high speed imposed by unpredictable tactical considerations.

Let us take the case of a K class destroyer embarking on a long hazardous journey from Alexandria to the meridian of Sirte and back. The rate of fuel consumption at 33 knots (full speed) is 14.7 tons per hour, whereas the rate at 13 knots (economical speed) is 2 tons per hour; ie at full speed it is more than seven times as much. Or, put a different way, the endurance range at 33 knots is only 1,040 sea miles compared with the 3,020 sea miles to be obtained at an economical speed of 13 knots. In the event, with much high speed manoeuvring likely in daylight hours during the 48 hour westward leg from Alexandria to the meridian of longitude 18°E, followed by 12 hours of skirmishing during aircraft attacks and two phases of surface ship action on the third day, more than half of the fuel could have been consumed, notwithstanding that all the uncertain return journey to Alexandria had yet to be covered.

A further factor complicating the problem was that Malta was so short of oil fuel that it was imprudent to consider sending ships in to fuel there, unless as in the case of the Hunts, it was also tactically necessary.

Although initially hampered by exceptionally stormy weather and heavy swell at the beginning of his return passage to Alexandria, Vian was anxious to diminish the hazards of the severe air attacks he expected would develop in Bomb Alley on the following day. Shortage of oil fuel in any one of his vessels could delay his whole force. He was well satisfied with the results of the battle in which he had forced Iachino to withdraw, without himself losing any of his force, and was certainly correct in deciding to return to Alexandria rather than risk the confusions and uncertainties of identification that must occur during a night attack in deteriorating weather.

The following table gives details of speed, fuel consumption, and range for certain classes of British destroyers in 1942, also the Hunts, and the *Dido* class of light cruisers. It can be seen that the *Didos* have an all round better endurance range than the destroyers and the Hunts, particularly at the lower speeds. The Hunts have a poor endurance range compared with the others at the lower speeds, while having a reasonably good range at high speed. It is evident, however, that the Hunts could barely get to Malta and back to Alexandria at anything in excess of 20 knots.

Class	Fuel capacity (tons)	Economical speed			Moderate Despatch			Despatch			Full speed		
		kts	tons per hr	range in miles	kts	tons per hr	range in miles	kts	tons per hr	range in miles	kts	tons per hr	range in miles
H	455	14	1.8	3,360	20	3.6	2,400	26	6.9	1,630	31	12	1,120
Tribal	520	10	1.7	3,110	20	4.3	2,440	25	7	1,840	33	16.3	1,050
J/K	490	13	2	3,020	20	3.85	2,420	28	8.6	1,520	33	14.7	1,040
L	567	10	1.8	3,080	20	4.4	2,560	25	7.3	1,950	33	17.6	1,060
Hunt II	277	10	1.2	2,350	20	3.2	1,730	25	6	1,140	26	7.2	1,000
Dido Cruisers	1,110	15	3.8	4,350	20	6.3	3,480	25	11.3	2,440	30.5	22.4	1,500

Radar Installations in British Ships at Sirte

All the *Didos* were commissioned with radar already installed, although the actual 'fit' depended upon availability. *Cleopatra* and *Dido* had Type 281 Air Warning radar and Type 285 AA fire control radar, *Euryalus* had Type 279, a Type 284 Surface fire control radar forward and a Type 285 aft, and also a pom-pom director ranging radar – Type 282. *Penelope* was fitted with 281, 284, and 285. *Carlisle,* like other C – Group AA conversions, had a Type 280 warning and fire control radar – this was derived from an Army gun-laying set.

The destroyer *Hero* had no radar: (see p53). The remaining destroyers, with three exceptions, were equipped with Type 286, a combined air and surface warning set derived from ASV 11. By 1942, a rotating frame aerial had been introduced, and thus the original limitations of the fixed array were largely overcome. The exceptions were *Lively, Legion,* and *Heythrop,* which were fitted with Type 285 as well as 286; and most of the Hunts would have been so equipped as these ships were given high priority for the AA radar.

On the subject of the use of radar in the Battle of Sirte, it must be remembered that there were no plan-position indicators in British ships at that time, and so a running plot of the short-range picture would have been impossible to maintain while watching the enemy ships and keeping an all-round look-out for hostile aircraft. Another limitation which rendered radar less useful for manoeuvring in company was the quantity of 'clutter' – sea returns – which obscured the screen out to 600 yards or more, depending upon the power output and frequency of the set, and also upon the state of the sea.

The captain of the *Penelope* writes: "We had been fitted with RDF but my experts had failed entirely to get it to work. As a matter of fact they reported triumphantly that it was at last working after our return to Malta after the battle. Half an hour later it was blown to smithereens by a near miss."

CHARACTERISTICS OF BRITISH NAVAL RADARS 1939 – 45

Type No		Wave-Length	Range (n.m)	Purpose
1938/ 39	79	7m	90/ 20,000	Air Warning, Cruisers & above
1941	271)			
	272)	10cm	10-25	Surface Warning:
	273)			Cruisers & above
	274	10cm	—	Surface Gunnery Control: 6in – 15in
	275	10cm	—	AA Gunnery Control: 4in – 4.5in
1944	277	10cm	25-35	Surface and Low Air Warning
1940	279	7m	90/ 20,000	79 with AA Barrage predictor
1939	280	3½m	nk	Air Warning/ Radar Ranging: Army Gun-Laying Mark 1 fitted to AA ships
1940	281	3½-4m	100/ 20,000	Air Warning (as 79)
1941	282)		3½	Close Range AA Gunnery Control

1942	283)	50cm	8½	Type 285 fitted for Barrage Control of main armament: 6in – 16in
1940	284)		10	Surface Gunnery Control: 6in – 16in
1940	285)		8½	AA Gunnery Control: 4in – 5.25in
1940	286	1.5m		Air Warning, small ships
1942	291	1.5m		286 replacement
1944	293	10cm	12½+	Air & Surface Target Indicating

APPENDIX L

Honours and Awards

It is not easy to devise a specific list of the honours for a particular operation, since they were often awarded for an accumulation of instances of outstanding performance and gallantry. The following list, mainly from a supplement to the *London Gazette* published late in the summer of 1942, appears to apply largely to Sirte, but may be incomplete.

"For courage, gallantry, skill, and seamanship in a brilliant action against strong enemy forces which were driven off and severely damaged. This action resulted in the safe passage to Malta of an important convoy."

KBE:
Rear-Adm Philip Vian
(immediate appointment after the action)

CB:

Capt G. Grantham	*Cleopatra*
Capt A. L. Poland	*Jervis*

CBE:

Capt A. D. Nicholl	*Penelope*

DSO (second bar):

Capt J. A. Micklethwait	*Sikh*

DSO (bar):

Capt E. W. Bush	*Euryalus*
Capt C. A. G. Hutchison	*Breconshire*
Capt D. M. L. Neame	*Carlisle*
Cdr J. H. Allison	*Kelvin*
Cdr P. Somerville	*Kingston*

DSO:

Capt H. W. U. McCall	*Dido*
Cdr C. T. Jellicoe	*Southwold*
Cdr P. D. H. R. Pelly	*Dido*
Engr Cdr S. J. Armstrong	*Dido*
Lt-Cdr J. T. B. Birch	*Hurworth*
Lt-Cdr W. F. N. Gregory-Smith	*Eridge*
Lt-Cdr R. H. Maurice	*Cleopatra*
Lt-Cdr W. N. Petch	*Dulverton*
Lt-Cdr Sir Standish O. G. Roche	*Beaufort*
Lt-Cdr P. A. R. Withers	*Avon Vale*
Lt-Cdr G. R. G. Watkins	*Havock*
Lt-Cdr A. Chancellor	*Kingston*

DSC (bar):

Lt-Cdr J. B. Laing	*Jervis*
Lt-Cdr A. S. Storey	*Cleopatra*
Lt G. J. Kirkby	*Kingston*
Lt J. S. Miller	*Penelope*
Mr E. A. Durnford	*Cleopatra*

DSC:

Lt-Cdr (E) I. G. Aylen	*Kelvin*
Lt-Cdr (E) A. H. Bacchus	*Lively*
Lt-Cdr (E) E. E. P. Freeman	*Sikh*
Surg Lt-Cdr B. S. Lewis	*Cleopatra*
Pay Lt-Cdr W. H. Field	*Cleopatra*
Lt G. R. A. Don	*Euryalus*
Lt P. Hankey	*Cleopatra*

Lt D. W. M. Macleod	*Southwold*
Lt D. L. Satterford	*Hasty*
Lt N. Scott-Elliott	*Zulu*
Lt D. A. Shaw	*Hurworth*
Lt R. F. Wells	*Jervis*
Lt J. L. West	*Carlisle*
Lt H. W. Stowell	*Dulverton*
Lt F. Smith	
Lt W. L. Crick	*Carlisle*
Lt W. McCall	*Eridge*
Lt D. S. Thorp	*Legion*
Lt (E) R. Andrewes	*Havock*
Lt (E) F. M. Philby	*Penelope*
Lt (E) A. Kennedy	*Breconshire*
Lt (E) H. R. Smith	*Carlisle*
Capt RM N. S. Boycott	*Cleopatra*
Sub Lt G. O. Graham	*Breconshire*
Sub Lt J. M. Elgar	*Beaufort*
Mr E. J. Brown	
Mr D. Macdonald	*Avon Vale*
Mr A. J. Stanton	*Kipling*
Mr F. D. Maynard	*Cleopatra*
Mr C. J. Rhodes	*Euryalus*
Mid B. W. Windle	*Dulverton*
Mid W. J. P. Greany	*Hero*

DSM (second bar):
CPO T. A. Topley
DSM (bar):
CPO R. P. Richards
CPO W. A. Savage
C Stoker H. A. Brooks

Bibliography

FIRST HAND ACCOUNTS: See Preface and Acknowledgements

OFFICIAL HISTORIES OF THE SECOND WORLD WAR:
Playfair, I. S. O.; *The Med and Middle East,* Vols II, III and IV, HMSO
Roskill, Captain S. W.; *The War at Sea,* Vols 1 and 2, HMSO

OTHER PUBLISHED WORKS:
Bragadin, Cdr Marc; *The Italian Navy in World War II,* USNI
Bush, Capt E. W.; *Bless Our Ship,* Allen & Unwin
Cunningham, Adm of the Fleet Viscount; *A Sailor's Odyssey,* Hutchison
Fraccaroli, A.; *Italian Warships of World War II,* Ian Allan
Edwards, Cdr K.; *Men of Action,* Collins
Kemp, Lt-Cdr P. K.; *HM Destroyers,* Herbert Jenkins
Lenton, H. T. and Colledge, J. J.; *Warships of World War II,* Ian Allan
Lenton H. T.; *British Fleet and Escort Destroyers of World War II,* Macdonald
Macintyre, Capt Donald; *The Battle for the Med,* Batsford
Pack, Capt S. W. C.; *Sea Power in the Med,* Arthur Barker
Pack, Capt S. W. C.; *Cunningham the Commander,* Batsford
Roskill, Capt S. W.; *The Navy at War,* Collins
Vian, Adm of the Fleet Sir Philip; *Action This Day,* Muller

Index

141

143